U. S. Department
of Transportation

**Federal Railroad
Administration**

Impact of Data Link Technology
on Railroad Dispatching Operations

Office of Research
and Development
Washington, DC 20590

U.S. Department of Transportation
Research and Special Programs Administration
John A. Volpe National Transportation Systems Center
Cambridge, MA 02142

Human Factors in Railroad Operations

DOT/FRA/ORD-04/11

Final Report
October 2004

This document is available to the
public through the National Technical
Information Service, Springfield, VA 22161.
This document is also available on the
FRA website at www.fra.dot.gov

REPORT DOCUMENTATION PAGE

1. AGENCY USE ONLY (*LEAVE BLANK*)	2. REPORT DATE October 2004	3. REPORT TYPE AND DATES COVERED Final Report September 1998 - October 1999

4. TITLE AND SUBTITLE Impact of Data Link Technology on Railroad Dispatching Operations	5. FUNDING NUMBERS R2103/RR204
6. AUTHOR(S) Nicolas Malsch, Thomas Sheridan, and Jordan Multer	

7. PERFORMING ORGANIZATION NAME(S) AND ADDRESS(ES) U.S. Department of Transportation Research and Special Programs Administration John A. Volpe National Transportation Systems Center Cambridge, MA. 02142	8. PERFORMING ORGANIZATION DOT-VNTSC-FRA-04-04

9. SPONSORING/MONITORING AGENCY NAME(S) AND ADDRESS(ES) U.S. Department of Transportation Federal Railroad Administration Office of Research and Development, Mail Stop 20 1120 Vermont Ave, NW Washington, DC. 20590	10. SPONSORING/MONITORING AGENCY REPORT NUMBER DOT/FRA/ORD-04/11

11. SUPPLEMENTARY NOTES

12a. DISTRIBUTION/AVAILABILITY STATEMENT This document is available to the public through the National Technical Information Service, Springfield, VA. 22161. This document is also available on the FRA web site at www.fra.dot.gov.	12b. DISTRIBUTION CODE

13. ABSTRACT (Maximum 200 words)

This study examined data link communication as an alternative channel to voice radio for railroad dispatchers. The goal was to compare how data link affected performance compared to voice radio only communications on measures related to safety, productivity, communication efficiency, and situation awareness. A data link system with two addressing options was compared to radio. The discrete message capability enabled the dispatcher to send a message to one individual at a time. The broadcast message capability enabled the dispatcher to send a single message to multiple recipients. The experiment was run on a human-in-the-loop railroad dispatcher simulator.

Overall, data link proved superior to the voice radio environment, in terms of safety. Safety of maintenance workers was improved by both data link systems while train safety was improved only for broadcast messages. No increase in dispatching productivity (train and track maintenance) was observed with data link. For communication efficiency, the results depended upon message complexity. Dispatchers spent less time exchanging simple messages with voice radio. Conversely, dispatchers exchanged complex messages more quickly in the data link environment. The differences in communication efficiency as a function of message complexity can be attributed to the type of interface: visual or auditory.

14. SUBJECT TERMS cognitive task analysis, radio communications, data link, decision-making, displays, intelligent railroad systems, railroad dispatcher, track allocation, train routing	15. NUMBER OF PAGES 76
	16. PRICE CODE

17. SECURITY CLASSIFICATION OF REPORT Unclassified	18. SECURITY CLASSIFICATION OF THIS PAGE Unclassified	19. SECURITY CLASSIFICATION OF ABSTRACT Unclassified	LIMITATION OF ABSTRACT Unclassified

METRIC/ENGLISH CONVERSION FACTORS

ENGLISH TO METRIC

LENGTH (APPROXIMATE)

1 inch (in) = 2.5 centimeters (cm)

1 foot (ft) = 30 centimeters (cm)

1 yard (yd) = 0.9 meter (m)

1 mile (mi) = 1.6 kilometers (km)

AREA (APPROXIMATE)

1 square inch (sq in, in^2) = 6.5 square centimeters (cm^2)

1 square foot (sq ft, ft^2) = 0.09 square meter (m^2)

1 square yard (sq yd, yd^2) = 0.8 square meter (m^2)

1 square mile (sq mi, mi^2) = 2.6 square kilometers (km^2)

1 acre = 0.4 hectare (he) = 4,000 square meters (m^2)

MASS - WEIGHT (APPROXIMATE)

1 ounce (oz) = 28 grams (gm)

1 pound (lb) = 0.45 kilogram (kg)

1 short ton = 2,000 pounds (lb) = 0.9 tonne (t)

VOLUME (APPROXIMATE)

1 teaspoon (tsp) = 5 milliliters (ml)

1 tablespoon (tbsp) = 15 milliliters (ml)

1 fluid ounce (fl oz) = 30 milliliters (ml)

1 cup (c) = 0.24 liter (l)

1 pint (pt) = 0.47 liter (l)

1 quart (qt) = 0.96 liter (l)

1 gallon (gal) = 3.8 liters (l)

1 cubic foot (cu ft, ft^3) = 0.03 cubic meter (m^3)

1 cubic yard (cu yd, yd^3) = 0.76 cubic meter (m^3)

TEMPERATURE (EXACT)

[(x-32)(5/9)] °F = y °C

METRIC TO ENGLISH

LENGTH (APPROXIMATE)

1 millimeter (mm) = 0.04 inch (in)

1 centimeter (cm) = 0.4 inch (in)

1 meter (m) = 3.3 feet (ft)

1 meter (m) = 1.1 yards (yd)

1 kilometer (km) = 0.6 mile (mi)

AREA (APPROXIMATE)

1 square centimeter (cm^2) = 0.16 square inch (sq in, in^2)

1 square meter (m^2) = 1.2 square yards (sq yd, yd^2)

1 square kilometer (km^2) = 0.4 square mile (sq mi, mi^2)

10,000 square meters (m^2) = 1 hectare (ha) = 2.5 acres

MASS - WEIGHT (APPROXIMATE)

1 gram (gm) = 0.036 ounce (oz)

1 kilogram (kg) = 2.2 pounds (lb)

1 tonne (t) = 1,000 kilograms (kg)

= 1.1 short tons

VOLUME (APPROXIMATE)

1 milliliter (ml) = 0.03 fluid ounce (fl oz)

1 liter (l) = 2.1 pints (pt)

1 liter (l) = 1.06 quarts (qt)

1 liter (l) = 0.26 gallon (gal)

1 cubic meter (m^3) = 36 cubic feet (cu ft, ft^3)

1 cubic meter (m^3) = 1.3 cubic yards (cu yd, yd^3)

TEMPERATURE (EXACT)

[(9/5) y + 32] °C = x °F

QUICK INCH - CENTIMETER LENGTH CONVERSION

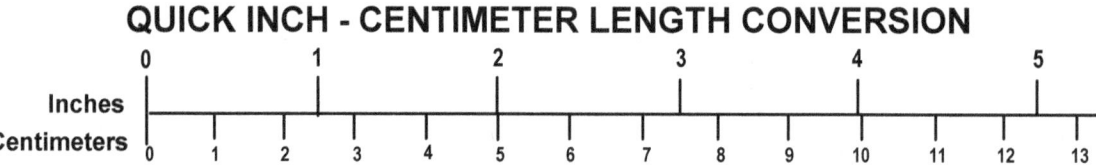

QUICK FAHRENHEIT - CELSIUS TEMPERATURE CONVERSION

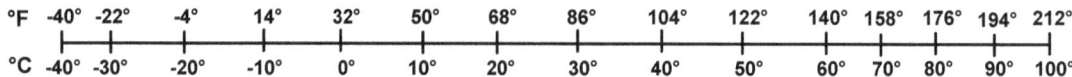

For more exact and or other conversion factors, see NIST Miscellaneous Publication 286, Units of Weights and Measures. Price $2.50 SD Catalog No. C13 10286

PREFACE

Voice radio channels have become increasingly congested as railroad traffic has increased and railroads centralize their operation centers. Dispatchers control increasingly large territories and their communication load has increased as a result. The ability of dispatchers to communicate effectively with train crews and roadway workers will impact the safety and productivity of railroad operations.

Digital (data link) communications systems can alleviate the burden of communication congestion by using a larger bandwidth, capable of displaying information in visual and auditory forms. The effectiveness of data link systems to assist dispatchers will depend upon how the interface is designed and the degree to which the design addresses human performance limitation and abilities. This report focuses on the safety, efficiency, and productivity issues associated with the introduction of a visually based (graphical and textual) data link interface for railroad dispatchers.

ACKNOWLEDGMENTS

This research was part of a program initiated by the Federal Railroad Administration (FRA) to examine the use of digital data link communications in the railroad environment. This work was performed as part of an ongoing research program at the John A. Volpe National Transportation Systems Center, in collaboration with the Human-Machine System Laboratory at the Massachusetts Institute of Technology (MIT). The FRA's Office of Research and Development supported this study, as part of its activities to develop intelligent railroad systems (Federal Railroad Administration, 2002).

The authors would like to thank Dr. Thomas Raslear of the FRA and Dr. Donald Sussman of the Volpe Center for their interest and support over the course of this research.

We also would like to express our deep gratitude to all the people who helped us during the past 2 years. Dr. Emilie Roth provided insightful comments on the dispatchers' strategies. Stephen Jones supported our study by making railroad dispatchers available to participate. John Pollard provided the expertise to solve many of our technical challenges. Sarah Miescher, Frank Sheelen, and Drew Kendra showed keen interest in our study and participated in many discussions. Santanu Basu provided the essential expertise to build and program the simulator. We thank Nicolas Oriol for his invaluable comments during earlier drafts of this study. Finally, we thank all the dispatchers who participated in our study, for their valued time and energy.

TABLE OF CONTENTS

SectionPage

Executive Summary ix

1. Introduction 1
1.1The Railroad Environment Today 1
1.2The Existing Environment of the Dispatcher 1
1.2.1The Dispatcher's Strategies 2
1.2.2Voice Radio Congestion 3
1.3Data Link Communication and the Dispatcher...3
1.4Research Goals 4
2. Method 5
2.1Overview 5
2.2Simulator Description 6
2.2.1The Dispatcher's Interface..6
2.2.2The Experimenter's Interface 7
2.2.3Equipment 8
2.3Routing Interface 8
2.4Communication Environments 11
2.4.1Voice Radio Environment...11
2.4.2Data Link Environment 11
2.4.3Discrete Data Link and Broadcast Data Link 14
2.5Scenario Description 15
2.5.1The Train Schedule 17
2.5.2The Hazard Schedule 17
2.5.3The MOW Schedule 17
2.6Experimental Design...18
2.7Participants..19
2.8Procedures 19
3. Results and Discussion 21
3.1Train Safety...21
3.2Mow Safety 22
3.3Communication Efficiency 23
3.3.1Performance Varies with Message Content 23
3.4Situation Awareness 28
3.5Productivity 29
3.6Dispatchers' Preferences...30
4. Conclusions 33
4.1Future Research 35
Appendix A. Message Trees 37
Appendix B. Event Schedules 43
Appendix C. Questionnaires 49
Appendix D. Experiment Documents..53

Glossary **59**

References..**61**

LIST OF FIGURES

Figure   Page

1. Simulator Configuration 6
2. Dispatcher's Workstation 7
3. Active Track Layout. 10
4. Dispatcher Message Console. 12
5. Dispatcher Message Menu Hierarchy 13
6. Preprogrammed Message 14
7. First Level of Experimenter's Message Tree 15
8. Track Layout 16
9. Number of Transactions by Time and Environment 24
10. Distribution of Transactions by Time and Type of Message 25
11. Mean Task Completion Time for Simple and Complex Type Messages by Communication
    Environment 26

LIST OF TABLES

Table   Page

1. Meaning of Track Color Coding 8
2. Menu Structure of Messages Initiated by Dispatcher 13
3. Territory Elements 15
4. Experimental Design 18
5. Safety of Trains and MOW Crews by Communication Environment 21
6. Mean Transaction Completion Time by Communication Environment 23
7. Characteristics for Selecting Modality in which to Present Information 27
8. Situation Awareness by Activity and Communication Environment 28
9. Productivity by Communication Environment 29
10. Dispatcher Ratings of Workload, Comfort, and Simulator Realism 30
11. Dispatcher Comments on the Use of Data Link 31

EXECUTIVE SUMMARY

The ability of dispatchers to communicate effectively with train crews and roadway workers impacts the safety and productivity of railroad operations. Voice radio channels have become increasingly congested as railroad traffic has increased and operations centers become more centralized. Data link represents a potential solution to supplement voice radio. Data link communication differs from voice radio because the information is digitally coded and discretely addressed. Digital coding allows many new options in providing communications better tailored to employee needs.

The additional channel capacity of data link will allow more information to be communicated. However, the use of data link poses challenges, as the dispatcher must be able to manage the new communications medium without experiencing information overload.

The goal of this study was to evaluate how data link affects dispatcher performance compared to the radio. Two data link environments were designed and evaluated against the current voice radio environment. The level of improvement was evaluated in terms of safety, efficiency, and productivity. Also examined were the dispatcher's attention allocation strategies.

Method

A visual (text-based) data link interface was designed as an alternative to the current voice radio communication environment. This data link system was compared to voice radio for common information transmissions using a railroad dispatcher simulator to evaluate its impact on dispatcher performance.

The data link interface was modeled after an e-mail application. To send a message, the dispatcher used a mouse to select from a set of message templates related to the task being performed. Keyboard entry was needed only to tailor the message. A data link system was designed with discrete and broadcast addressing capabilities. The discrete message capability enabled only private "one to one" communications in which the dispatcher could send a message to a single recipient. The broadcast message capability enabled the dispatcher to send a single message to multiple recipients.

The dispatcher's workstation enabled the dispatcher to route trains and communicate with workers in the field. The dispatcher used two or three monitors depending on the communication environment. Two of these monitors displayed the track layout (routing interface), and one served as the dispatcher's data link display (communication interface). In the voice radio environment, a two-way radio was used in place of the data link display. The dispatcher interacted with the routing (track layout) monitors using a mouse. For the data link display, a keyboard and mouse were used. For communication in the data link condition, the dispatcher used only the data link interface to initiate communication requests or to reply to people in the field.

Two scenarios were designed using 15 scheduled trains in each. To evaluate safety, each scenario included two types of hazards: trespassers on the track and children stoning the train. Each scenario also included maintenance-of-way (MOW) activities. Using the track layout screens, the dispatcher routed trains, blocked track, cleared routes, and took other actions to control equipment in the field.

The following three safety measures were collected: percent of trains alerted in response to a hazardous event, the percent of MOW crews properly protected, and situation awareness scores. The questionnaire was divided into four groups of questions: routing, hazards, MOW activities, and communications.

To evaluate communication efficiency, total transaction time was measured. Total transaction time represented the duration of a transaction between the dispatcher and the respondent. A single transaction could include multiple exchanges of information.

MOW activity and the "on time" performance of the routed trains were evaluated. The number of late trains entering the stations were recorded, as well as the number of trains that were more than five minutes late. MOW activity was evaluated by recording the number of granted MOW requests.

The participants were six professional dispatchers: one woman and five men. Three participants had 7 to 9 years dispatching experience, while the other three had less than 2 years. Participants were paid the same hourly rate they received for performing their usual job duties.

Each dispatcher participated in two scenarios, with a different communication environment each time. Before each trial, dispatchers were trained on the interface they would use. After the experiment, there was a short debriefing session. Each trial lasted one hour, and was interrupted once after 30 minutes so the participant could complete a situation awareness questionnaire. The participant's task was to perform their usual dispatching task given the constraints imposed by the new environments. At the conclusion of each scenario, the dispatcher completed a brief questionnaire.

Data Link Improves Communication

Our results suggest that data link can improve communication efficiency, safety, and situation awareness. The differences between conditions were not always statistically significant, but in almost every case, they favored data link. Compared to voice radio, both data link systems improved safety and situation awareness. For productivity, no differences were observed between data link conditions and voice radio.

With data link, dispatchers protected a greater percentage of trains and MOW crews as compared to the radio. By providing information in a visual format, data link eliminated readback errors and hearback errors associated with the auditory modality. Translating track requests from alphanumeric text to a graphic display on the track layout display made the request even easier to process. The visual presentation of information in the data link systems minimized the demand placed on the dispatcher's memory. Anecdotal comments by the participants suggested it also reduced stress by giving the dispatcher the opportunity to respond to messages when time allowed, providing a quieter environment in which to work.

The advantage of communicating information in visual form was evident in the evaluation of situation awareness. Situation awareness for data link was better than voice radio for routing, hazard awareness, and communication. While the dispatcher devoted more resources to processing visual information with data link than with radio (there were three displays to monitor, instead of two), no adverse impact was evident. MOW activity was the only category in which performance was as good or better than the radio condition. Dispatchers had a visual form of information to assist them in situation awareness.

Overall, the differences between the discrete data link condition and the broadcast data link condition were small. The broadcast version showed a greater improvement in train safety than the discrete version. The broadcast version minimized communication workload by providing a simple way to reach multiple recipients, allowing the dispatcher to attend to other tasks. For example, the dispatcher could use a single message to alert all trains along a particular branch, while the discrete system required the dispatcher to contact each train individually.

Communication efficiency for voice radio and data link varied as a function of the characteristics of each medium. Information communicated by voice radio was presented in an auditory format. Information communicated via data link was presented in a visual format. Each form proved better suited for presenting some kinds of information than others.

Voice radio proved better suited to communicating short and informal communications as well as time-critical messages that required immediate action (i.e., a dispatcher reporting no speed restrictions when a locomotive engineer called to request a temporary speed-restriction bulletin, or alerting a locomotive engineer to the presence of a trespasser). For these types of communications, data link doubled the communication times over voice radio. These results were due to the auditory format in which the information was presented.

In this experiment, data link was better suited for communications whose length or complexity imposed a significant burden on memory. In railroad operations, these characteristics are typical of safety critical messages that require formal acknowledgement procedures (i.e., granting a Foul Time request or authorizing a train movement using a Form D). Data link provided an efficient channel for these communications. As a result, communication times were reduced by a factor of two. The concept of not having to repeat a message multiple times was also appealing to the dispatchers in our study.

In the voice radio and data link conditions, the performance differences observed between the two types of messages were due to the modality or format in which the information was presented, not the communication medium. While information sent over voice radio is presented in an auditory form, digital communications systems like data link provide more options for presentation. Data link supports both auditory and visual modalities.

The differences identified between radio and data link also depended upon the details of how each interface was implemented. Had the data link interface required the dispatcher to make heavier use of the keyboard to enter messages than with the current design, the results might have been quite different. Successful implementation of a data link interface will depend upon applying principles of good human factors design and usability testing to meet the needs of dispatchers who use this communication interface.

The current study suggests that dispatchers benefit from both voice and data link communication modes. In recommending the conditions under which each medium should be used, this study suggests that voice radio is best suited for communicating simple, time-sensitive messages to one recipient. Data link system is best suited for communicating lengthy messages. Sending discrete messages works best where privacy is important or the message content would benefit only the recipient for which the message is intended. Sending broadcast messages works best when there is a need to communicate the same information to multiple recipients.

1. INTRODUCTION

1.1 The Railroad Environment Today

Railroad traffic has increased in recent years. As a result, railroads have improved their infrastructure by investing in faster trains and new technologies to enhance train movements. Between 1992 and 1995, railroads bought more than 800 new locomotives (Railroad Facts, 1996). The Federal Railroad Administration (FRA) and the railroad industry are working together on the development of intelligent railroad systems that include new computer and communications technologies in train control and the scheduling of railroad operations (FRA, 2002).

One consequence of these changes is the movement toward more efficient communication. Dispatchers must work closely with train crews and roadway workers to manage track use. Managing the communication process is a challenge, given the current voice radio channel availability. Using voice radio as the primary communication channel in the railroad environment has resulted in communication congestion. Data link communication can provide capabilities not available through voice radio. However, the use of data link itself poses challenges, as the dispatcher must be able to manage the additional communications.

Currently, the dispatcher acquires information from parties in the field by way of voice radio and telephone. By what criteria will a dispatcher select the communication medium, when data link becomes available for sending and receiving information? What kind of information is appropriate for each medium? To address these questions it is important to first understand how the dispatcher acquires and shares information in the current environment. To begin answering these questions, the current communication environment of the dispatcher was analyzed.

1.2 The Existing Environment of the Dispatcher

Railroad dispatchers are responsible for managing track use, ensuring that trains are routed safely and efficiently, and ensuring the safety of the maintenance-of-way (MOW) personnel working on and around the track (Devoe, 1974). These tasks require integrating multiple sources of information, projecting track use into the future, and balancing multiple demands from various sources. The railroad dispatcher is responsible for the safety of people and equipment on the track as well as the efficient use of railroad resources. By contrast, in the aviation environment, these two job functions are divided between the air traffic controller whose primary concern is safety and the airline dispatcher whose primary concern is productivity.

Successful performance of the train routing task depends on the ability of the dispatchers to monitor train movements beyond their territory, balance multiple demands placed on track use, and factor in unplanned events in allocating track. This requires monitoring train positions and MOW activities. In CTC territories, the dispatcher monitors train position via signals communicated by track circuitry, on a visual display (i.e., a computer display or mimic board) and monitors events through two-way radio communications with railroad crews in the field. In territories, where information about train position is not available (either Automatic Block Signal territory or dark territory), the dispatcher must rely upon voice radio communications with railroad personnel in the field as the only means to monitor train movements.

1

Voice radio traffic places significant demands on the dispatcher's attention and memory. To stay informed and in control the dispatcher performs a variety of tasks. These tasks include: answering requests, determining the current state of railroad operations (delays, speed restrictions, and track outages), informing railroad entities of the current state of operations, coordinating with other railroad "supervisors" (e.g., train masters and yard masters), and filling out paperwork.

These tasks contribute to three types of demands on the dispatcher:

- Demands on attention associated with monitoring the radio channel and responding to radio requests.

- Demands on memory, associated with the need to keep track of many more elements than the ones actually displayed on the routing or communication interface.

- Demands on decision-making strategies associated with the assignment of track to trains or MOW crews.

1.2.1 The Dispatcher's Strategies

Dispatchers have developed several strategies for meeting their job demands (Roth, Malsch and Multer, 1999). Awareness of dispatcher strategies is important for designers considering new aiding technologies. Strategies can signal problems in the current dispatching environment that dispatchers are compensating for, and may suggest ideas for new aids. When introducing new technologies, designers need to be careful not to inadvertently create conditions that prevent the dispatchers from implementing their strategies, especially if there is no replacement strategy.

One strategy consists of off-loading memory requirements. A great amount of information needs to be considered when making track allocation or routing decisions. Some of this information can be found in rulebooks, schedules, memos, and daily bulletins. Dispatchers have developed techniques to extract key pieces of information in a more accessible form. One example is the "cheat sheet," which is a piece of paper summarizing the most relevant information in the schedule. Another example is the desk book, a clipboard including formal memos, speed bulletins, scheduled track outages, or informal notes written by the dispatcher. Both tools provide the dispatcher with a convenient way of keeping track of changes and updates.

A second set of strategies is to anticipate unplanned events and plan ways to address these events. These strategies include coordination with the dispatchers for abutting territories and from the people in the field (i.e., asking adjoining dispatchers about changes in the usual routing and alerting them to changes caused by unplanned events). The dispatcher develops a "game plan" to work out meets and passes depending on train schedules and priorities for each shift and territory ahead of time. Dispatchers may summarize parts of the game plan in their cheat sheets. To maintain the "big picture" they monitor activity beyond their territory. If an overview display showing track use for all territories is available, they monitor where trains are on the track even before they enter their territory. Dispatchers also take advantage of the party line feature of the voice radio. Dispatchers listen for information on the radio channel not directly addressed to them. This information can provide important clues to potential delays or problems. Typically, dispatchers listen for "train out of station" messages, equipment problems, (when a locomotive engineer is talking to the mechanical department), and other dispatcher commitments that might have an impact on their territories.

Dispatchers plan by developing contingencies for unplanned events such as engine failures and late or unscheduled trains. Planning includes taking advantage of the windows of opportunity for track usage. If track that was previously in use becomes available earlier than expected, dispatchers will call up a MOW crew to let them know it is available. In the same manner, they will call locomotive engineers before a train is scheduled to leave the station to give them the speed bulletin for the trip.

A third strategy is to level workload. Dispatchers try to shift the work from high workload periods to lower workload periods. For example dispatchers will pre-name trains, clear routes in anticipation of needs, and give provisional authority (giving track away until further notice). Other methods include reducing the amount of communication (especially for work crews), and performing multiple tasks in parallel (e.g., clearing a route for a train and answering the radio for a MOW person).

1.2.2 Voice Radio Congestion

There was consensus among the interviewed dispatchers that the voice radio channel is often overloaded. Furthermore, there was agreement that voice radio is not well suited for some communication tasks. For example, long dialogues intended to convey detailed information such as exact location, should be conducted on a more private voice channel (i.e., telephone).

1.3 Data Link Communication and the Dispatcher

Data link technology provides an alternative that can supplement voice radio and telephone communications. Data link communication differs from voice radio because the information is digitally coded. This makes it possible to discretely address individual receivers or multiple recipients.

Data link would benefit the railroad industry by making data available in real time, while improving information in terms of quantity, reliability, and quality (Vanderhorst, 1990). Real time transmission of information could improve the dispatcher decision-making process. The contribution of real time information can be understood when one observes the current dispatching environment. For example, at one dispatching center, with passenger trains comprising the majority of traffic, the system shows delays for each train. However, the information is not displayed in real time. As a result, the dispatchers cannot rely on this information for time-critical decisions. They need to solicit additional sources of information and use strategies for allocating track that depends upon a coarser level of information. Current data link technologies could help.

Additional channel capacity of data link means that more information can be communicated. However, increasing the amount of data could lead to information overload. To use the new technology efficiently, data link must provide additional data that can be turned into useful information. Information normally provided aurally could be displayed visually. This feature would assist dispatchers in managing their workload.

Data link also has the potential to address the voice radio congestion problem. Data link will reduce congestion in the radio environment by providing an alternative, higher bandwidth communication channel. Currently, only one person can transmit over a given voice radio channel. When someone transmits a message, other parties are blocked from transmitting their messages over the same channel. Data link enables many people to transmit multiple messages

3

simultaneously. Data link may also change the order in which messages are answered. Currently, the order in which messages are answered depends upon the dispatcher's implicit, situationally dependent priority. The ability to store and display messages will require that messages are organized to facilitate the dispatcher's tasks. This organization can make explicit (observable) the dispatcher's priorities. Thus, data link changes the nature of the communication problem for the dispatcher. Instead of answering messages in the order they arrive, now the dispatcher or the system must prioritize the order in which messages are answered. In the current radio environment, the dispatcher faces a similar situation because there are several frequencies over which people can communicate. Data link highlights this challenge for the dispatcher. Designers will need to consider ways to help the dispatcher prioritize the order in which messages are answered.

Data link also provides the ability to design flexible interfaces (either visual or aural) for delivering information. However, the success of this communication channel is likely to depend upon its implementation. Simply adding data link technology without considering how information will be presented may create new problems. Advantages present in the current voice radio environment can be lost if designers do not understand their importance.

Using data link, information can be presented aurally or visually. Each modality has advantages and disadvantages. What information should be sent via data link and what information should be communicated by voice? This study seeks to answer this question by examining how data link affects railroad dispatcher performance. As the focal point for communications in the railroad control environment, the benefits and drawbacks of implementing data link in the dispatcher's working environment were investigated.

1.4 Research Goals

The goal of this study was to evaluate how data link affected dispatcher performance compared to the current voice radio channel. Using a railroad dispatcher simulator, two data link environments were designed and evaluated against the current voice radio system. The level of improvement in terms of safety, efficiency, and productivity within this new environment was evaluated. The dispatcher's attention allocation strategies were also examined.

2. METHOD

2.1 Overview

The performance differences between data link and voice radio were measured using a human-in-the-loop railroad dispatcher simulator. In the voice condition, messages were communicated by two-way radio. Transactions communicated by radio were synchronous; the transaction between sender and receiver took place at the same point in time. Use of a voice radio channel by a sender blocked its use by other potential senders. Therefore, a message could only be sent by one person at time. However, anyone in range of the communication could listen to the message.

A user interface for a data link system was created to operate similarly to an email system. The dispatcher interacted with the data link system using a computer monitor, keyboard, and mouse. Unlike voice radio, the data link system was asynchronous. Transactions communicated by radio were asynchronous; transactions between senders and receivers could take place at different points in time. The sender of a message could send a message to one recipient or to many recipients.

Although a real-world system would have both capabilities, in the current study, these two ways of sending messages were separated into two experimental data link conditions to evaluate their impact on dispatcher performance. The two data link conditions were called discrete and broadcast. In the discrete condition, messages were sent to a single recipient. In the broadcast condition, messages were sent to multiple designated recipients. Each type of message distribution has advantages and disadvantages. Sending a single message to multiple recipients in one transaction by the dispatcher requires less work than sending the same message multiple times. The challenge is determining who received the message. For safety critical transactions, the dispatcher needs confirmation that the recipient received the message. Sending messages to recipients who don't need this information may overload the recipients with unnecessary information. Conversely, failing to send it to a recipient who should have received this information could contribute to a mishap.

In the two data link conditions, voice radio was not used. The two communication environments were evaluated separately to identify the effects of each communication environment on dispatcher performance.

Dispatchers performed their normal duties routing trains and allocating track to maintenance of way (MOW) crews. Each participant was exposed to two scenarios in which a variety of events occurred such as trespassers on the tracks, delayed trains, and requests from track personnel for Foul Time. Participant performance was measured in terms of efficiency (minimizing communication time), productivity (minimizing train delays and maximizing maintenance work), safety (avoiding collisions), and attention allocation.

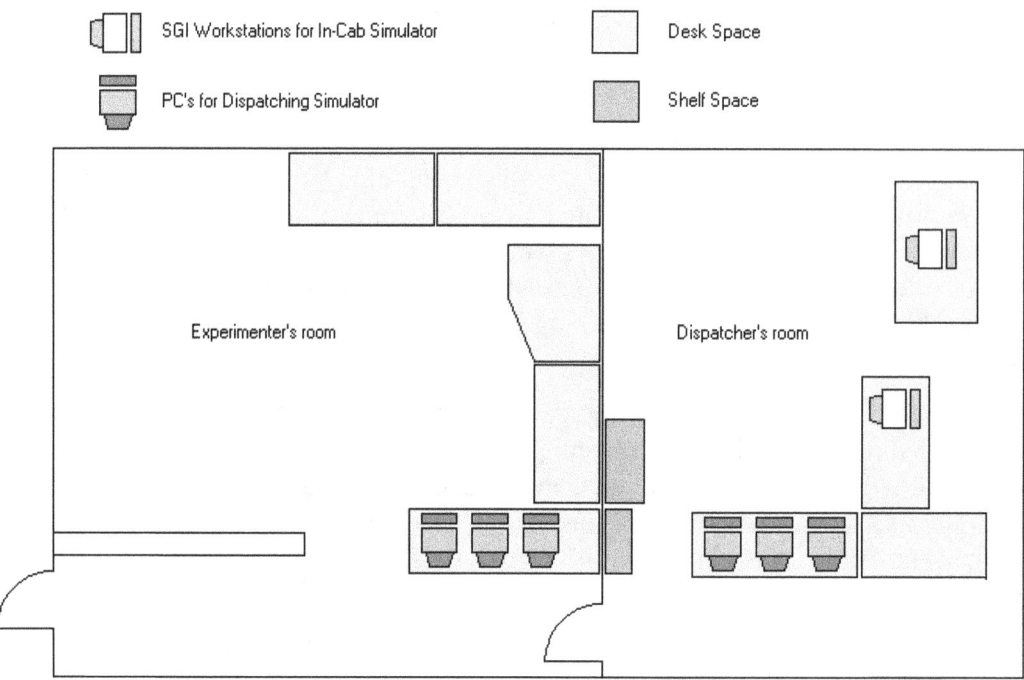

Figure 1. Simulator Configuration

2.2 Simulator Description

The simulator was divided into two parts as shown in Figure 1: the dispatcher's workstation and the experimenter's workstation. Each workstation was composed of two display elements, reflecting the two main activities of the dispatcher: routing and communication. The routing interface displayed the track layout and was modeled after a Central Traffic Control (CTC) based signal system. It simulated routing activity for a track network on the Northeast Corridor. The communication interface was either a portable two-way radio or a data link display, depending on the experimental condition.

2.2.1 The Dispatcher's Interface

The dispatcher's workstation enabled the dispatcher to route trains and communicate with workers in the field. The dispatcher used two or three monitors depending on the communication environment. Two of these monitors displayed the track layout (routing interface) and one served as the dispatcher's data link display (communication interface) as seen in Figure 2. In the voice radio environment, a two-way radio was used in place of the data link display. The dispatcher interacted with the routing (track layout) monitors using a mouse. For the data link display, a keyboard and mouse were used.

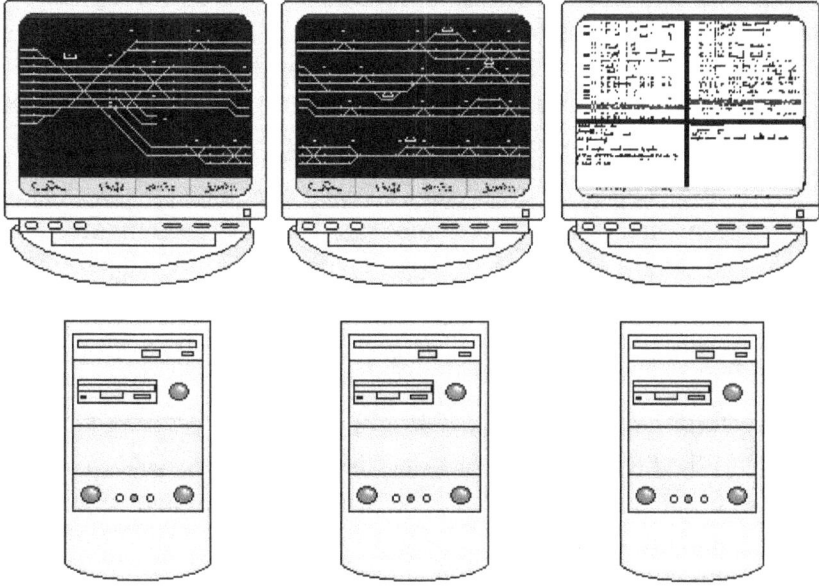

Figure 2. Dispatcher's Workstation

Using the track layout screens, the dispatcher routed trains, blocked track, cleared routes, and took other actions to control equipment in the field. For communication in both data link environments, the dispatcher used the data link interface to initiate communication requests or to reply to people in the field.

2.2.2 The Experimenter's Interface

The experimenter's workstation enabled the experimenter to monitor the experiment and to play the roles of other entities with whom the dispatcher would interact. These entities included: train crews, MOW crews, yardmasters, trespassers, and other dispatchers. For example, the experimenter could halt, reverse direction, or derail a train. Although the experimenter's workstation consisted of the same three monitors as the dispatcher's workstation (as shown in Figure 2), the experimenter's workstation did not allow dispatching activities. The experimenter controlled the routing interface and data link interface with the appropriate keyboard and mouse.

Two monitors displayed the track layout. The third monitor displayed the data link interface. In the radio environment, the experimenter used three portable radios in place of the data link display. Playing the role of other railroad staff involved the use of assistants communicating with each other and the dispatcher about events taking place.

In the data link environment, the experimenter used the message console to communicate with the dispatcher. Preprogrammed messages were created to play the part of other railroad operating personnel. However, the type of preprogrammed messages differed from those available to the dispatcher. In the voice radio environment, the experimenter(s) still used the message console because it provided the appropriate message to read aloud on the radio. For more details about the operation of the simulator, see Basu (1999).

7

2.2.3 Equipment

The railroad dispatcher simulator was comprised of six personal computers (PCs) connected via a local area network (LAN), and a set of four portable radios. Each was a Windows™ based machine with a Pentium™ II class processor. Seventeen-inch cathode ray tube (CRT) type monitors were used. The simulation was programmed using Java™.

The dispatcher's workstation consisted of three PCs. The experimenter's workstation was located in an adjacent room, and consisted of three PCs. The three PCs in the dispatcher's room were connected via a LAN to the three PCs in the experimenter's room. The experimenter initiated actions or created conditions to which the dispatcher responded. Alternatively, the experimenter, playing the role of locomotive engineer, roadway worker, or another dispatcher, responded to events or action initiated by the dispatcher.

Four Motorola HT/MT1000 portable radios were used to simulate voice radio communication. One radio was present in the dispatcher's room, and the experimenter and two assistants used the remaining three radios. In the voice radio condition, three people simulated the communications of the operating personnel amongst themselves and with the dispatcher. A video camera located in the participants' room recorded all experimental trials.

2.3 Routing Interface

The routing simulation was modeled on an Amtrak passenger railroad dispatching system. It showed a color-coded track display with text to display the current track state.

Color-coding - The color of individual track segments (referred to as blocks) represented how the track was allocated. The color-coding conformed to the conventions as seen in Table 1.

Table 1. Meaning of Track Color Coding

Color	Meaning
Red	Indicates the presence of a train. Other trains are not allowed in this block.
Green	Cleared route. Train has permission to enter this block.
Blue	Indicates track work is occurring. Trains are not allowed to enter without permission of MOW workers.
White	Track is currently unallocated.

Text information - Train numbers were displayed above the track if traveling outbound and below the track if traveling inbound. Inbound trains had even numbers and outbound trains had odd numbers. In addition, an arrow was located on the left or on the right of the train number to indicate travel direction. Finally, a plus or minus sign was displayed on the left of the train number to indicate whether the train was ahead of or behind schedule. This display was only updated when a train passed an interlocking. Stations and interlockings were named.

Track layout - The track consisted of a terminal station named Boston, with ten platforms from which four branches departed towards New York City as shown in Figure 3. The four branches, labeled A, B, C, and D respectively, varied in length and number of stations.

8

Routing activities - The main routing tasks were accomplished using mouse-activated buttons located at the bottom of the screen; clearing and unclearing a route as well as blocking and unblocking tracks. Clearing a route enabled a train to move over that section of track. Other trains were prohibited by the signal system from entering track sections occupied by the train. Unclearing a route made the previously cleared track available for other uses. The track uncleared automatically after the train went through. The unclearing delay typically encountered by dispatchers when correcting a mistake was not implemented. If a switch was changed while the train was in an interlocking, the change did not affect the train's movement. A two-aspect signal system (clear route or route occupied) was implemented. The dispatcher blocked a track to enable roadway workers and their equipment to occupy the track. Unblocking the track removed this protection for the roadway worker crew and equipment and made the track available for train movements or other MOW crews. The simulator propagated the state of the signal to the adjacent block. Hence, trains slowed down and eventually stopped if a cleared route was not available.

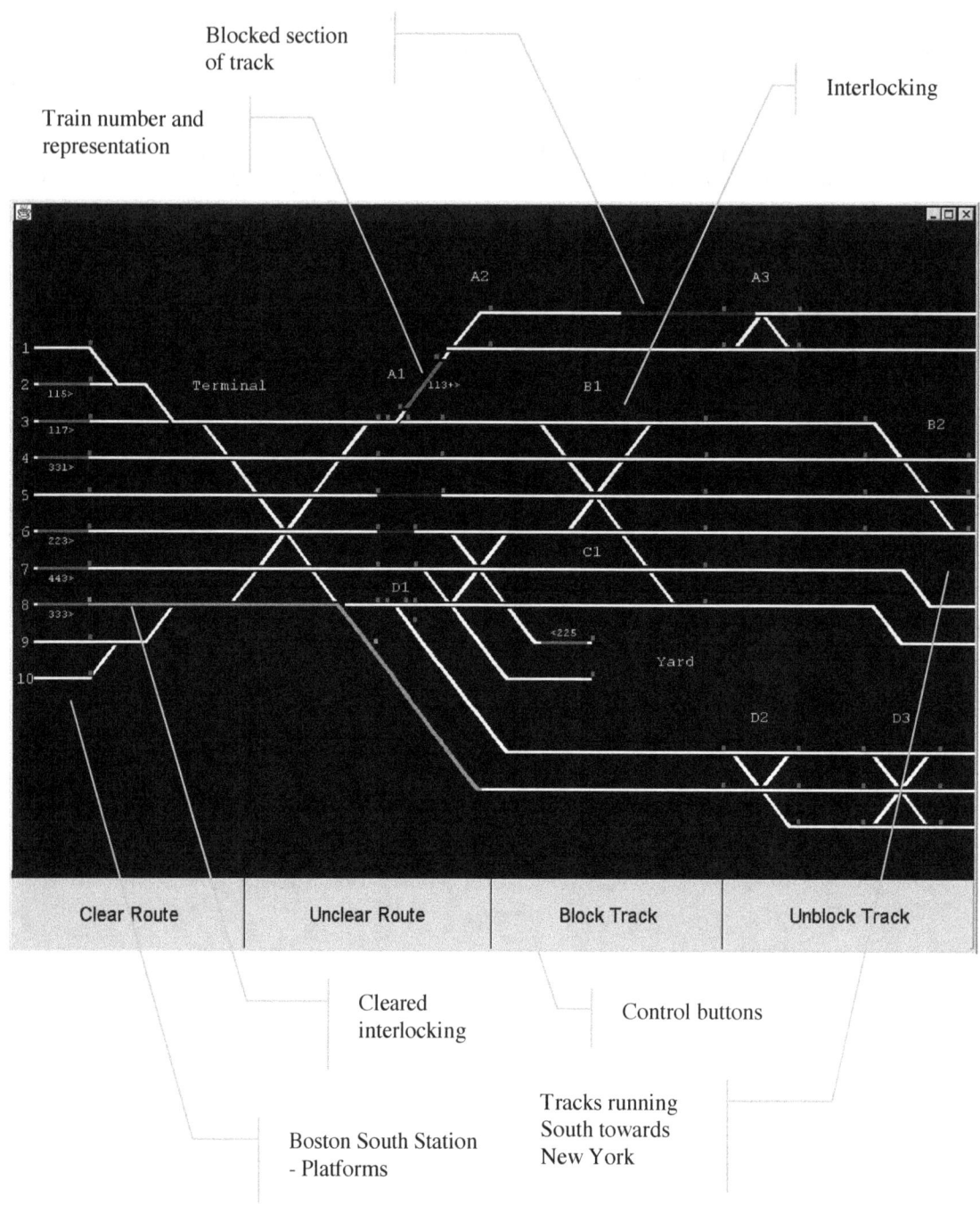

Blocked section
of track

Train number and
representation

Interlocking

Cleared
interlocking

Control buttons

Boston South Station
- Platforms

Tracks running
South towards
New York

Figure 3. Active Track Layout

2.4 Communication Environments

2.4.1 Voice Radio Environment

The experimental communication procedures were modeled after a communication protocol used at a scheduled train operations dispatching center. Messages transmitted to the dispatcher were computer generated in accordance with the dispatcher's routing decision. If the simulator was programmed to act on the presence of a trespasser within a given time span, and the dispatcher was routing a train through the area where the trespasser was, the simulator would then send a message to the experimenter. The experimenter, playing the role of the locomotive engineer on that particular train, then called the dispatcher on the radio to warn of the trespasser's presence. If the dispatcher routed no trains through the territory while trespassers were supposedly present there, these trespassers went unnoticed by the dispatcher.

Communications were not always directed to the dispatcher. To simulate communications among field personnel, the experimenter and several assistants used a set of computer-generated cues to talk amongst themselves using the three radios. The experimenters used the same communication protocol as the dispatcher.

2.4.2 Data Link Environment

The data link environment was displayed visually using an e-mail-like interface. The data link interface contained a menu of preprogrammed messages. The voice radio was unavailable in the data link conditions. The data link interface consisted of a monitor with a mouse and keyboard for information input. To send a message, the dispatcher used a mouse to select from a set of message templates (containing text) relating to the task being performed. Keyboard entry was needed only to tailor the message. This approach minimized the need for time-consuming keyboard use. Two ways of sending messages using the data link system were designed: discrete and broadcast. The discrete message capability enabled only private "one to one" communications in which the dispatcher could send a message to a single recipient. The broadcast message capability enabled one to many communications in which the dispatcher could send a message to multiple recipients. The screen was split into four windows as shown in Figure 4.

Received messages window - The upper left window of Figure 4 displays the list of received messages. With each incoming message, an additional line was added to the list specifying the sender. Messages were sorted by arrival time. If unselected, messages were preceded by a series of four question marks. Once highlighted, messages were preceded by a series of stars. If the dispatcher used the reply button to answer a message, the message was preceded by a series of "Rs."

Text message window for received messages - The lower left window of Figure 4 displays the entire text of the selected message. If this message referred to a track location, this location was highlighted in yellow on the track layout display.

Received message window Sent message window

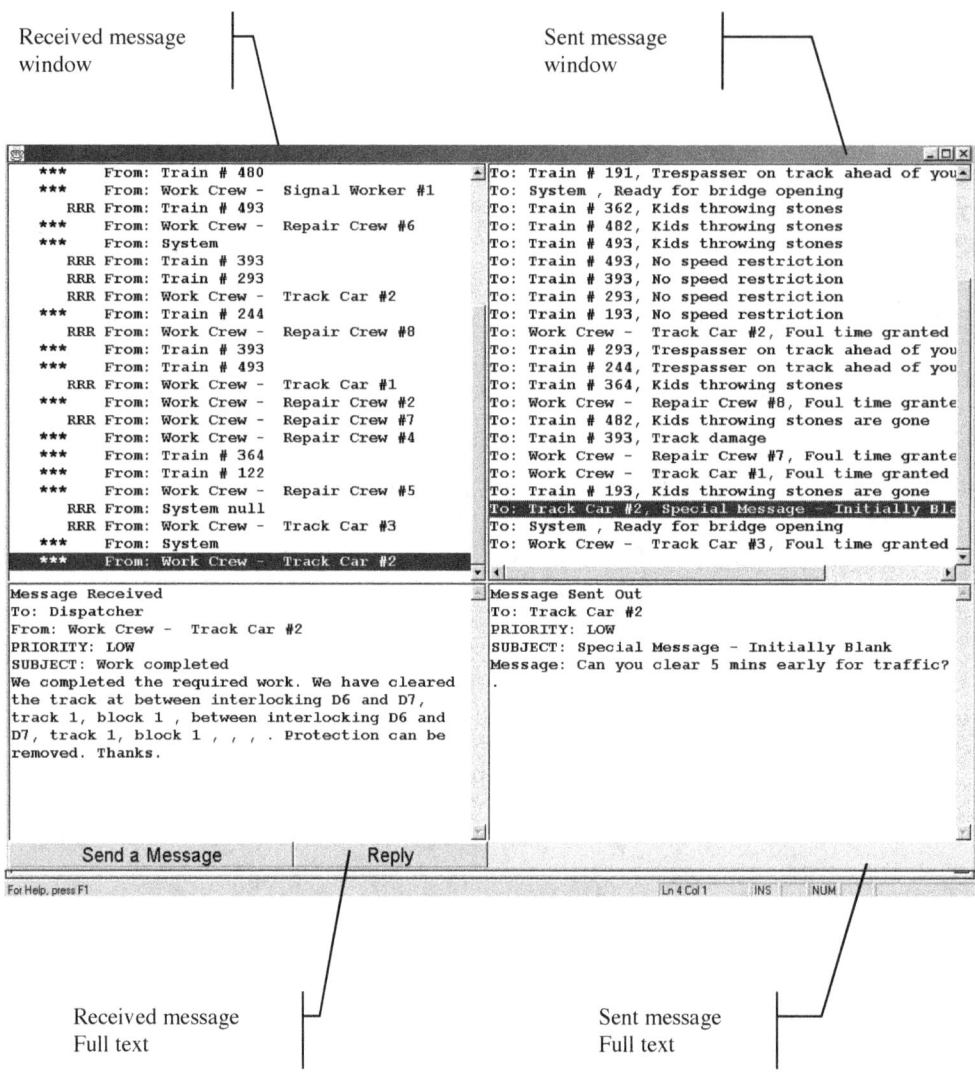

```
 ***     From: Train # 480                     To: Train # 191, Trespasser on track ahead of you▲
 ***     From: Work Crew -   Signal Worker #1   To: System , Ready for bridge opening
 RRR From: Train # 493                          To: Train # 362, Kids throwing stones
 ***     From: Work Crew -   Repair Crew #6     To: Train # 482, Kids throwing stones
 ***     From: System                           To: Train # 493, Kids throwing stones
 RRR From: Train # 393                          To: Train # 493, No speed restriction
 RRR From: Train # 293                          To: Train # 393, No speed restriction
 RRR From: Work Crew -   Track Car #2           To: Train # 293, No speed restriction
 ***     From: Train # 244                      To: Train # 193, No speed restriction
 RRR From: Work Crew -   Repair Crew #8         To: Work Crew -   Track Car #2, Foul time granted
 ***     From: Train # 393                      To: Train # 293, Trespasser on track ahead of you
 ***     From: Train # 493                      To: Train # 244, Trespasser on track ahead of you
 RRR From: Work Crew -   Track Car #1           To: Train # 364, Kids throwing stones
 ***     From: Work Crew -   Repair Crew #2     To: Work Crew -   Repair Crew #8, Foul time grante
 RRR From: Work Crew -   Repair Crew #7         To: Train # 482, Kids throwing stones are gone
 ***     From: Work Crew -   Repair Crew #4     To: Train # 393, Track damage
 ***     From: Train # 364                      To: Work Crew -   Repair Crew #7, Foul time grante
 ***     From: Train # 122                      To: Work Crew -   Track Car #1, Foul time granted
 ***     From: Work Crew -   Repair Crew #5     To: Train # 193, Kids throwing stones are gone
 RRR From: System null                          To: Track Car #2, Special Message - Initially Bla
 RRR From: Work Crew -   Track Car #3           To: System , Ready for bridge opening
 ***     From: System                           To: Work Crew -   Track Car #3, Foul time granted ▼
 ***     From: Work Crew -   Track Car #2
```

```
Message Received                          Message Sent Out
To: Dispatcher                            To: Track Car #2
From: Work Crew -   Track Car #2          PRIORITY: LOW
PRIORITY: LOW                             SUBJECT: Special Message - Initially Blank
SUBJECT: Work completed                   Message: Can you clear 5 mins early for traffic?
We completed the required work. We have cleared   .
the track at between interlocking D6 and D7,
track 1, block 1 , between interlocking D6 and
D7, track 1, block 1 , , , . Protection can be
removed. Thanks.
```

| Send a Message | Reply |

For Help, press F1   Ln 4 Col 1   INS   NUM

Received message Full text   Sent message Full text

Figure 4. Dispatcher Message Console

Sent message window - The upper right window in Figure 4 displays the list of outgoing messages. With each sent message, another line was added to the list. Each line contained the recipient and the subject of the message.

Text message window for sent messages - The lower right window shown in Figure 4, displays the entire text of the message the dispatcher highlighted in the sent message window. This text window lacked the track location-highlighting feature.

Message creation: the dispatcher's message-tree - To facilitate message creation, the most frequently used message types were preprogrammed. The dispatcher scrolled within a hierarchical menu to select a message. The menu contained a small number of fundamental messages. Clicking the reply button or the send message button at the bottom of the received-messages window displayed a menu. The menu consisted of a four level tree, through which the sender proceeded in sequence, from level one to level four. The menu hierarchy is shown in Table 2 and Figure 5.

12

Table 2. Menu Structure of Messages Initiated by Dispatcher

Level	Content	Example
1	Message Priority	High, medium or low
2	Recipient	Engineer, MOW
3	General subject	Trespasser, Kids throwing stones
4	Detailed message content	Track Work – Foul Time Granted
		Track Work – Foul Time Refused

Clicking a button in the fourth level of the message tree hierarchy displayed a window with the desired message. If the dispatcher wanted to send a message not found in the message tree, a "blank message" could be created.

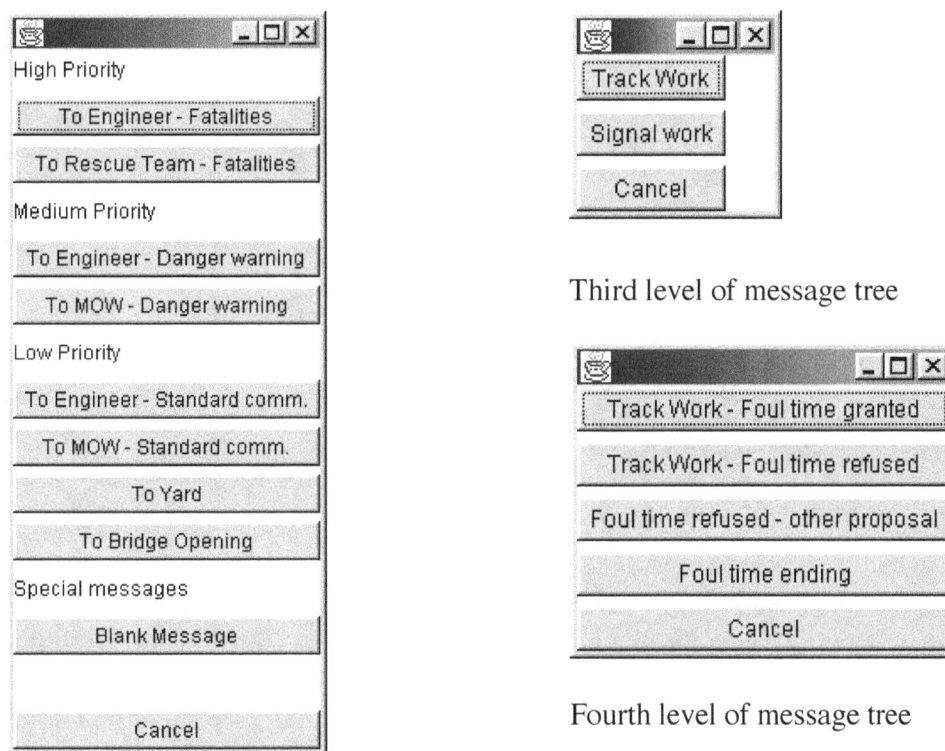

First two levels of message tree

Third level of message tree

Fourth level of message tree

Figure 5. Dispatcher Message Menu Hierarchy

The entire dispatcher message tree used in the data link environments is shown in Appendix A. To complete a message, the dispatcher filled in the blanks using the mouse or keyboard (see Figure 6). Typically, the dispatcher filled in a location, time, and train number. To specify location or train number, the dispatcher used the mouse. By selecting the location or train number on the track layout display, the blank fields in the message were completed automatically. Once a field was filled in, the cursor moved to the next blank field. In the final step, the dispatcher pressed the send button to deliver the message. Once sent, messages were always acknowledged.

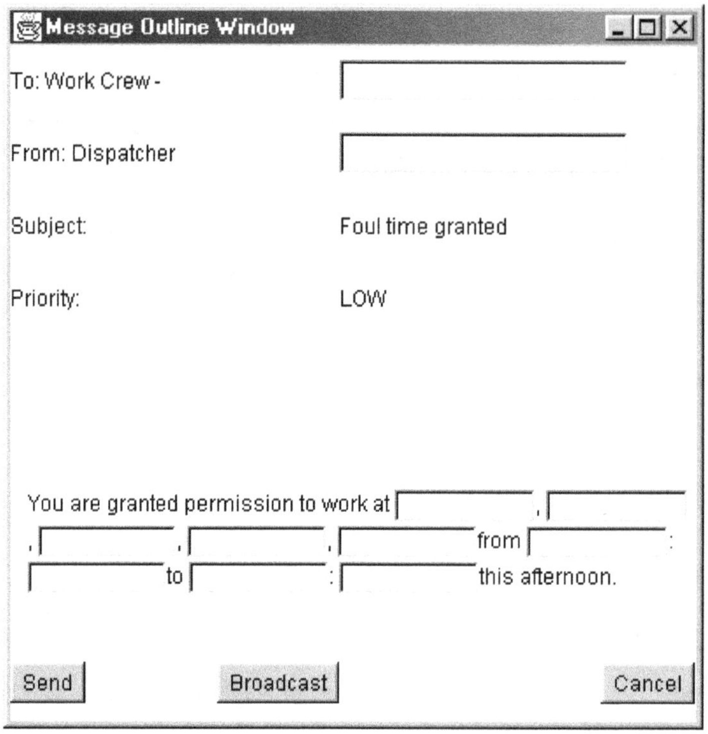

Figure 6. Preprogrammed Message

2.4.3 Discrete Data Link and Broadcast Data Link

With the discrete data link condition, messages were sent to only <u>one</u> recipient. In the broadcast data link condition, messages were always sent to <u>multiple</u> recipients. To send a message, the dispatcher specified one primary recipient and a group of secondary recipients (see Appendix A for the list of the groups). It was assumed that recipients always properly acknowledged messages.

The experimenter's data link interface was identical to the dispatcher's message console. To create a message, the experimenter used the same procedure as the dispatcher. However, the experimenter had message trees available for all railroad entities such as a dispatcher tree, an engineer tree, a MOW tree, and a "miscellaneous" tree as shown in Figure 7. The message trees were similar in structure to the previously described dispatcher message tree. The experimenter message tree can be found in Appendix A.

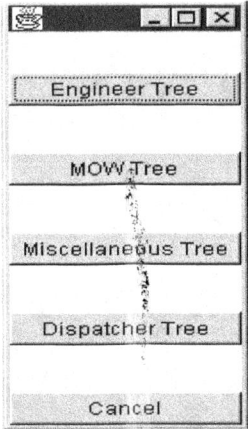

Figure 7. First Level of Experimenter's Message Tree

2.5 Scenario Description

Two scenarios were designed. Each experimental run started at the beginning of a new shift and lasted one hour. Figure 8 represents the territory for which the dispatcher was responsible. The territory for both scenarios was the same. The territory contained the elements shown in Table 3. The top track layout shows the terminal on the left. The track at the right side of the top track layout is located south of the track to the left. On the bottom display, the left side of the track layout continues the display shown on the right hand side of the top track layout.[1]

Table 3. Territory Elements

Territory Elements
Four branches: A, B, C, D
One Terminal station
Four intermediate stations: A, BL, BR, D
One drawbridge (not displayed, between D7 and D8)

---

[1] The track is not displayed to scale.

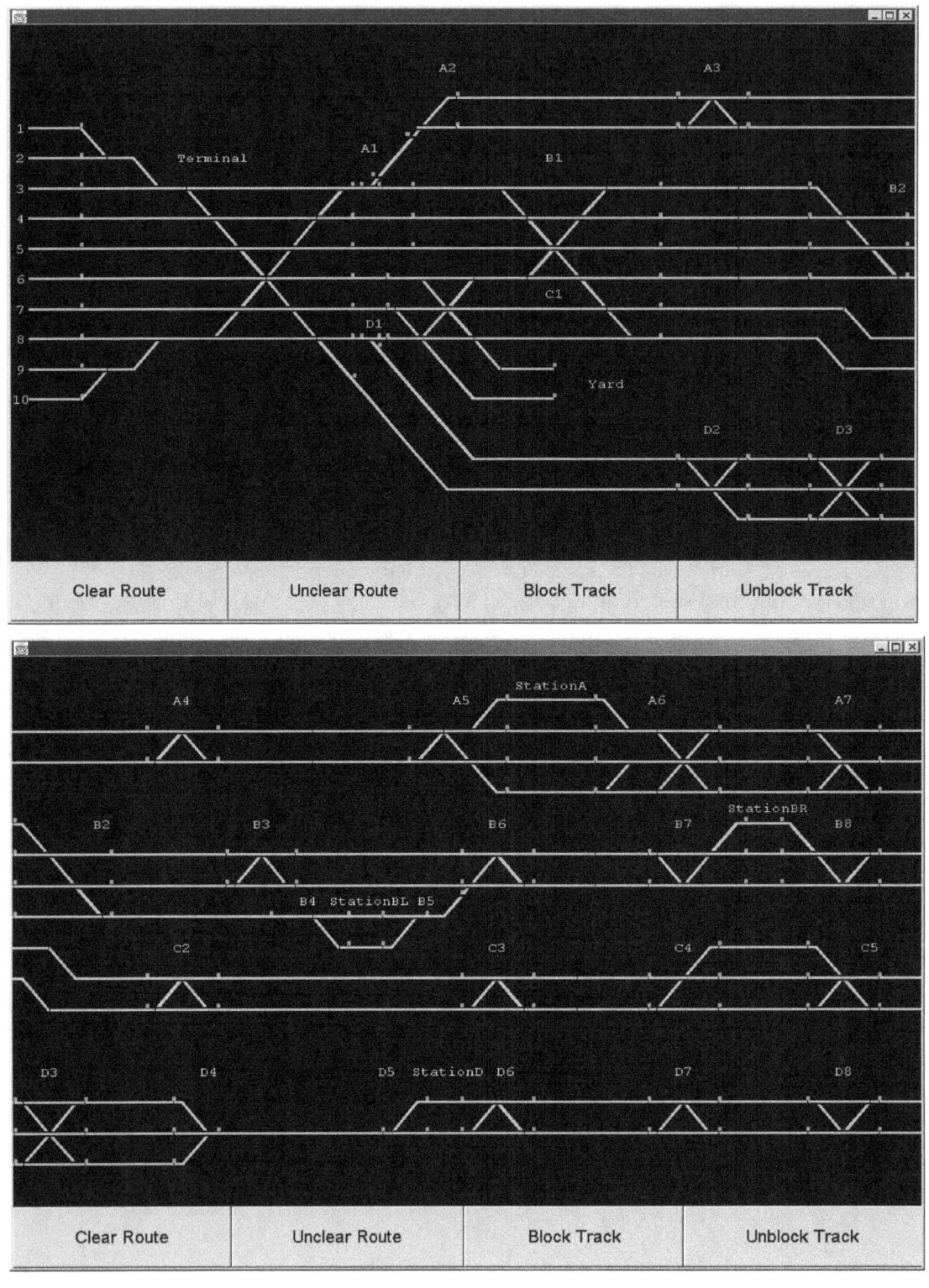

Figure 8. Track Layout

2.5.1 The Train Schedule

Fifteen scheduled trains were used during each scenario. The schedule and the territory were designed so that if the dispatcher routed the trains perfectly, all trains could arrive on time or slightly early. If the dispatcher made a significant routing mistake (i.e., forgetting about a train for five minutes or longer), the affected train could not make up for the delay. Small routing mistakes (one or two minutes) did not appear in the data. This was done to simulate the fact that engineers will try to make up for their delays. During the experiment, dispatchers had a copy of the schedule readily available.

Trains outside of the stations were moving when the simulation began. All trains were on time and had sufficient track to move at full speed for the first three minutes of the simulation without any action by the dispatcher. The entire train schedule is shown in Appendix B.

2.5.2 The Hazard Schedule

To evaluate safety, two types of hazards were used; each scenario included five hazards. The first type of hazard was the presence of trespassers on the track. Two or three times during each experiment, trespassers were present on the track for a certain period. If during that period of time a train passed through the area, the locomotive engineer saw the trespassers and the dispatcher was alerted. The dispatcher was expected to relay the trespasser alert to all other trains that would travel through that area. The second type of hazard was children stoning the train, which occurred twice during each experiment. If trains were routed into the hazardous area at the "right" time, the dispatcher was alerted and had to relay the information to the other trains near the hazard.

To collect enough data, these two types of hazards were scheduled to take place in an area with heavy train traffic. The appropriate hazard occurrence time was chosen so that delays between five and ten minutes would not prevent the experimenter from gathering enough data. The territory was busy enough and the hazard schedule designed to account for variations in routing. For details on the hazard presence times and on the expected "alerter trains," see Appendix B.

2.5.3 The MOW Schedule

Each scenario included MOW activities. To provide enough data points to compare performance between conditions and to create a moderately stressful workload, the number of MOW requests a dispatcher would normally face was exaggerated. After preliminary testing, 12 track requests were made during each scenario. These 12 requests included:

- 2 bridge lifting requests
- 2 management-scheduled track outages
- 8 unscheduled MOW requests

At the beginning of each experiment, the dispatcher took over the protection of two MOW crews who were granted permission by the previous dispatcher on the shift.

There were two types of unscheduled MOW activity. The first activity was signal work. Signal workers requested protection for work on the signals near an interlocking. The second type of activity was track work. Track work was requested and performed either by track cars (special trucks riding on the track and checking its condition) or by repair crews. In the data link case, there were two different answer messages, one for each type of MOW crew. Dispatchers were expected to use the appropriate reply message, depending on the type of request. In the radio condition, dispatchers were instructed to use the "Form D" movement authority for all MOW requests.

The MOW schedule was designed to create challenging "meets and passes" problems for the dispatcher. At least one MOW request could not be granted if all trains were on time. Appendix B shows the MOW schedule.

2.6 Experimental Design

The type of communication environment was the independent variable. There were three levels: radio, discrete data link (DD), and broadcast data link (BD). The experimental design is shown in Table 4. A balanced incomplete block design (Lindman, 1992) was used. All dispatchers started with a data link scenario.

Table 4. Experimental Design

Dispatcher	Environment		
	Radio	**Data link**	
		Discrete	**Broadcast**
1	Scenario 1	Scenario 2	
2	Scenario 2	Scenario 1	
3	Scenario 1		Scenario 2
4	Scenario 2		Scenario 1
5		Scenario 1	Scenario 2
6		Scenario 2	Scenario 1

The dependent variables (i.e., measured variables) can be classified into three groups:

- Safety
- Efficiency measurements of the communication system
- Productivity

Safety Measures

Three safety measures were collected. Two measures related to action taken by the dispatcher to warn or protect trains and MOW crews. The third safety measure concerned situation awareness. The two safety measures related to warning or protecting trains and MOW crews were: the percent of trains alerted in response to a hazardous event, and the percent of MOW crews properly protected.

In the first safety measure for each hazard, a fixed number of trains were supposed to receive a warning message. For each train properly warned, the dispatcher earned one point.[2] All scores were converted into percentages.

---

[2] The dispatcher could alert trains that did not need alerts. Participants received no credit when this event occurred, nor were they penalized.

The second safety measure was the number of MOW crews protected properly when Foul Time or Form D movement authority was granted. For each MOW request granted, the pieces of track asked for and the pieces of track given away were recorded. When MOW people were protected, the dispatcher earned one point. The number of points varied with each dispatcher. The percentage of MOW crews protected was calculated by dividing the number of properly protected MOW crews by the number of MOW requests granted for each dispatcher.

The third safety measure was situation awareness, which was evaluated using the Situation Awareness Global Assessment Technique (SAGAT) developed by Endsley (1993). During the experiment, the simulation was paused so that the participant could complete a questionnaire. The questionnaire was divided into four groups of questions: routing, hazards, MOW activities, and communications questions. A dispatcher received one point for each correct answer. Partial credit was given if the answer was partially correct. For details about the questionnaire, see Appendix C.

Communication Efficiency

To evaluate communication efficiency, total transaction time was measured. Total transaction time represented the duration of a transaction between the dispatcher and the respondent. A single transaction could include multiple exchanges of information. The duration was measured from the time at which an initial message was received by the dispatcher to the time at which final response was sent by the dispatcher.

In the radio environment in this experiment, the initiation of the message and reception occurred simultaneously. In the data link environment, a delay could occur between the time the message was displayed on the monitor and the time the dispatcher observed and read the message. In the data link condition, the time at which the message was displayed on the monitor represented the initiating event for measuring total transaction time. The transaction was considered complete in the radio environment when the dispatcher completed the verbal response. In the data link condition, the transaction was completed after the message was sent and the experimenter forwarded the message to the appropriate recipient.

Productivity Operations

MOW activity and the "on time" performance of the trains were evaluated. The number of trains entering a station was known for all dispatchers. The number of late trains entering the stations were recorded, as well as the number of trains that were more than five minutes late. MOW activity was evaluated by recording the number of granted MOW requests.

2.7 Participants

The participants were six professional Amtrak dispatchers: one woman and five men. Three participants had 7 to 9 years dispatching experience. Three others had less than 2 years experience. Participants were paid at the same hourly rate they received for performing their usual job duties.

2.8 Procedures

Each dispatcher was present in the laboratory for six to eight hours. Each dispatcher participated in two scenarios, with a different communication environment each time. Before each trial, dispatchers were trained on the interface they would use. After the experiment, there was a short debriefing session.

A short training program was designed to familiarize each participant with the simulator and the communication environments they would experience. The training consisted of two phases. In the first phase, the dispatcher learned how the simulator operated (approximately 30 minutes). During the second phase of training, dispatchers learned the schedule (approximately 90 minutes).

The voice radio communication equipment was different from what participants were accustomed to and so training was given. In the data link environments, training was necessary to introduce the dispatcher to the data link interface, to gain familiarity with the message tree and learn the rules (when to alert a train and how to alert it). During this first training phase, the experimenter explained the routing procedures. On a training scenario, the dispatcher practiced routing trains (with eight trains, four inbound trains and four outbound trains, and a yard move). Then, the experimenter walked the dispatcher through the voice radio or the data link system. Next, the participant practiced routing and communicating on the training scenario modified by adding hazards and MOW requests. During this training, the experimenter sat next to the dispatcher to answer questions about the system. Dispatchers were given the structure of the message tree in written form (Appendix A).

During the second phase, the experimenter prepared the dispatcher for the experimental trials. The experimenter trained each dispatcher on the schedule for the next scenario. Dispatchers were given up to an hour and a half to become familiar with the schedule by practicing with the routing part of the simulator. Familiarization training was repeated before the second trial, as the scenario was different.

Just before the experiment began, the experimenter reviewed all the rules (transmission rules for voice radio and message handling for data link) with the dispatcher. The participant was allowed to use any notes prepared during the training. The document showing the structure of the message tree, and the Form Ds were made available. The documents provided to the dispatchers in addition to the schedule for each scenario can be found in Appendix D.

Each trial lasted one hour and was interrupted once after 30 minutes to complete the situation awareness questionnaire. The participant's task was to perform their usual dispatching task given the constraints imposed by the new environments. At the conclusion of each trial, the dispatcher completed a brief questionnaire. Dispatchers were asked to evaluate workload, comfort with the system, and the usefulness of data link. Questionnaires for all three environments can be found in Appendix C. After completing the second trial, the dispatcher also answered some open-ended questions about the two environments and ranked the environments by preference.

3. RESULTS AND DISCUSSION

3.1 Train Safety

Train safety was evaluated by calculating the ratio of actually alerted trains to the number of trains that needed to be alerted. Table 5 shows these ratios for each communication environment.

Table 5. Safety of Trains and MOW Crews by Communication Environment

Safety Measure	Voice Radio (%)	Environment	
		Data link	
		Discrete (%)	Broadcast (%)
Trains Alerted	33	45	93
MOW crews protected	64	94	97

The broadcast data link was the safest environment. The percent of trains alerted was highest in the broadcast condition, followed by the discrete data link environment and the radio environment. The differences observed between the broadcast data link case and the two other conditions were statistically significant ($t_{(6)} = 6.02$, p.< .05 comparing discrete to broadcast data link and $t_{(6)} = 9.36$, p.< .05 comparing voice radio to broadcast data link). The better performance of the broadcast data link case was due to the ease with which multiple designated trains could be notified. In this environment, dispatchers were free to broadcast the alerting message to all trains on one branch or to all trains on their territory. Thus, the dispatcher could alert all trains entering the hazardous area with only one message. The drawback of the broadcast environment was that forgetting to send one alert message endangered multiple trains. In one case, a dispatcher neglected to warn trains of a hazard, which resulted in 20 percent of the trains failing to receive the warning. A second drawback could occur if warnings resulted in false alarms. If the train never encountered the trespasser, but received the warning, the crew might give less credence to this type of warning in the future.

In the radio and discrete conditions, the dispatcher alerted each train individually. If the dispatcher was busy when notified of the hazard, the dispatcher might delay alerting some or all of the trains. The differences between the voice radio and discrete data link condition were not statistically significant. Although the differences were not statistically significant, the direction of the differences favors the discrete condition. Dispatchers alerted a greater percentage of trains in the discrete data link condition than in the voice radio condition. The train closest to the hazardous area was notified in 83 percent of the cases for the voice radio, and 100 percent of the cases in the discrete environment. In the voice radio environment after alerting the closest train, the dispatchers may have allocated their attention to other tasks and forgotten to alert the other trains. Alternatively, the dispatcher's criterion for which trains should be notified in the voice radio condition may have differed from their criterion in the discrete data link condition. The dispatcher may have decided that only some trains traveling on a specific branch were at risk and therefore only notified the trains perceived to be at risk.

21

3.2 Mow Safety

Dispatchers normally control the entire track territory for which they are responsible. However, when maintenance is necessary on or near the track, dispatchers give temporary control of the track section to the MOW crew. To make sure the track section under repair is protected, the dispatcher blocks that track section so that other trains are denied permission to enter. Trains cannot enter the protected track without the permission of the MOW crew. However, sometimes there is confusion about the exact track section the MOW crew requests. For example, where there are two tracks the MOW crew may request authority to work on track one, but the dispatcher may inadvertently give them authority to work on track two. Alternatively, after receiving permission to work on a section of track, the MOW crew may inadvertently work on unprotected track instead of the protected track. Both of these situations can compromise safety for the MOW crew.

The number of MOW crews properly protected during each experiment was recorded. Whenever dispatchers blocked the track requested or a portion of track greater than requested, MOW crews were assumed safe. A dispatcher who granted a track request, but failed to physically block the track, resulted in an unprotected MOW crew. Table 5 shows the results in percentages for each environment. In the voice radio environment, 24 MOW crews were protected properly out of 37. In the discrete environment, 29 MOW crews were protected properly out of 31, and in the broadcast environment, 25 out of 26 MOW crews were protected properly.

Both data link systems were clearly superior to the voice radio communication environment. The differences observed were statistically significant ($t_{(6)} = 5.98$, p. $< .05$ comparing voice radio to discrete data link and $t_{(6)} = 7.32$, p. $< .05$ comparing voice radio to broadcast data link). The two data link environments did not exhibit a significant difference. In the voice radio condition, the process of listening to a track request and transcribing it was time-consuming and error prone. If the voice radio transmission was unclear, the dispatchers asked the sender to repeat the message. If an error was detected during the initial transmission or during the acknowledgement, the process was repeated. Dispatchers made errors in hearing and transcribing the message. These kinds of errors are typical of the errors that occur in voice radio environments. They have also been documented in the aviation environment (Monan, 1983; Monan 1988; and Golaszewski, 1989).

In the data link conditions, the MOW foreman (represented by the experimenter in our study) requested authority to work on selected portions of the track by sending an email message to the dispatcher. The location and duration of the track request was displayed in a text format. The location was also displayed on the track layout display, color-coded in yellow.

Errors in the data link environment usually came from a peculiarity of track layout interface. When the dispatcher viewed a message requesting work authority on a particular section of track, the track layout interface displayed this information by showing the requested track section in yellow. When a dispatcher granted a MOW crew's authorization to work on a track section (blocking the track for use by others), the track section was color-coded blue on the track layout display. If the request message was still displayed in the text message window of the data link interface, the operator could not see if the track was properly blocked because the yellow color-coding of the MOW request masked the blue color-coding of the granted authorization.

The results illustrate that a visual display has the potential to improve safety by minimizing data entry errors and reducing memory load for the recipient. However, the details of how the interface is implemented will also impact safety.

3.3 Communication Efficiency

The average transaction time for each environment was calculated. The results are summarized in Table 6. Lower transaction times were observed for the two data link environments, compared to the radio. The difference observed between the broadcast data link environment and the voice radio environment was statistically significant ($t_{(157)} = 2.28$, p < .05, comparing voice radio to broadcast data link). The difference between the discrete data link and the voice radio condition was not statistically significant, although the trend was in the same direction as the broadcast data link condition.

Table 6. Mean Transaction Completion Time by Communication Environment

| | Environment | | |
| | | Data link | |
	Voice Radio	Discrete	Broadcast
Mean Transaction Time (s)	227	174	135

3.3.1 Performance Varies with Message Content

To understand why transaction times were lower for both data link conditions, the distribution of messages by transaction time was examined. Figure 9 shows the distribution of message transactions by time. For all three conditions, the majority of transactions were completed in two minutes or less. In each condition, there were a small number of messages that took longer to complete. For the voice radio condition, there were more of these lengthy transactions compared to the data link conditions. In the voice radio environment, the percentage of messages completed after five minutes was 85 percent. By contrast, in the data link conditions the percentage of messages processed was 97 percent or greater. Thus, some messages took longer to communicate in the voice radio condition. Similarly, 9 percent of messages were never answered (presumably forgotten) in the voice radio condition. By contrast, in the data link conditions, dispatchers forgot significantly fewer messages. None of the messages were forgotten in the broadcast condition, and only 1 percent of the messages were forgotten in the discrete condition.

The difference between voice radio and data link may be partly explained by the additional memory load required to process messages in the voice radio condition. Dispatchers were heard asking at least once during each voice radio condition, "Who was that on the voice radio a couple of minutes ago?" In the data link interface, the visual display provided an easy way to remember who called.

23

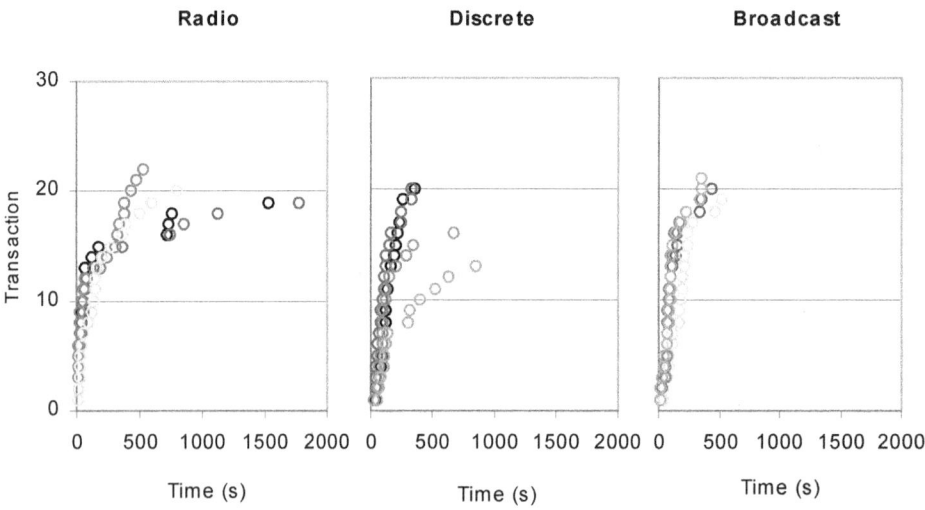

Figure 9. Number of Transactions by Time and Environment

To understand what type of message might account for the longer transaction time, messages were divided into categories by content. Figure 10 shows the transaction time distribution by the type of message. The message types included: denied MOW requests, granted MOW requests, messages between train crews and the dispatcher, miscellaneous messages, and messages that were not forwarded. Figure 10 shows that granted MOW requests accounted for the difference between the data link conditions and the voice radio condition. There were a comparatively large number of granted MOW requests that took longer than 500 seconds compared to the two data link conditions.

To clarify the distinction between message types and communication efficiency in the three communications environments, the communication transactions were separated into two types depending on the type of answer. The first type of communication, referred to as simple communications, included denied MOW requests (i.e., Foul Time), requests for bulletins on temporary speed restriction bulletins (TSRBs) when there were none, and the hazard alerts communications. The second type of communications called complex communications included only one type of communication - granting a MOW request. In each environment, simple and complex messages were compared and transmitted as a function of time. Figure 11 shows the average transaction time for the two communication types by environment.

24

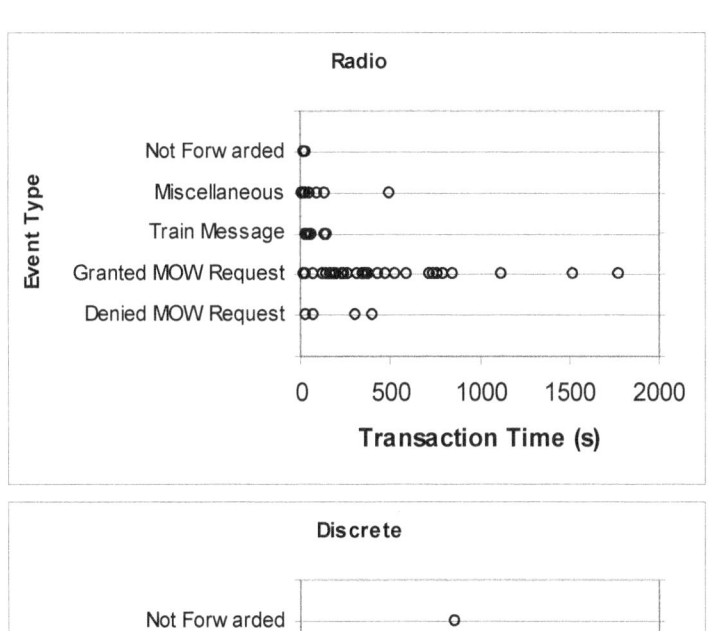

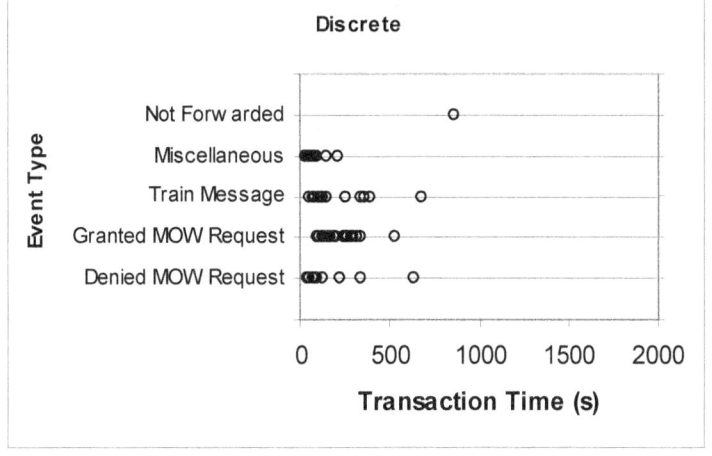

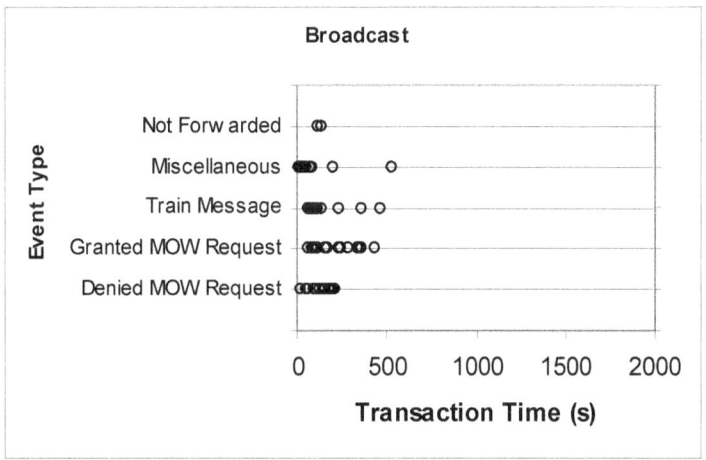

**Figure 10. Distribution of Transaction by Time and
Type of Message**

As expected, in all three environments the average transaction time was shorter for simple messages than for complex ones. For simple messages there were statistically significant differences between the voice radio condition and the two data link conditions ($t_{(90)}$=3.36, p < .05 comparing voice radio and direct data link and $t_{(100)}$ = 2.48, p < .05 comparing voice radio to broadcast data link). In both cases, the transaction times were lower in the voice radio condition.

25

The average transaction time was 62 seconds in the voice radio condition compared to 111 seconds in the discrete data link condition, and 161 seconds in the broadcast data link condition. For complex messages, the voice radio condition performed worse than the two data link conditions. The average transaction time was 463 seconds in the voice radio condition compared to 199 seconds in the discrete data link condition, and 197 seconds in the broadcast data link condition. Again, these differences were statistically significant ($t_{(55)}$ = 3.07, p. < .05 comparing voice radio to discrete data link and $t_{(53)}$ = 2.95, p. < .05 comparing voice radio to broadcast data link). There were no statistically significant differences between the discrete and broadcast conditions.

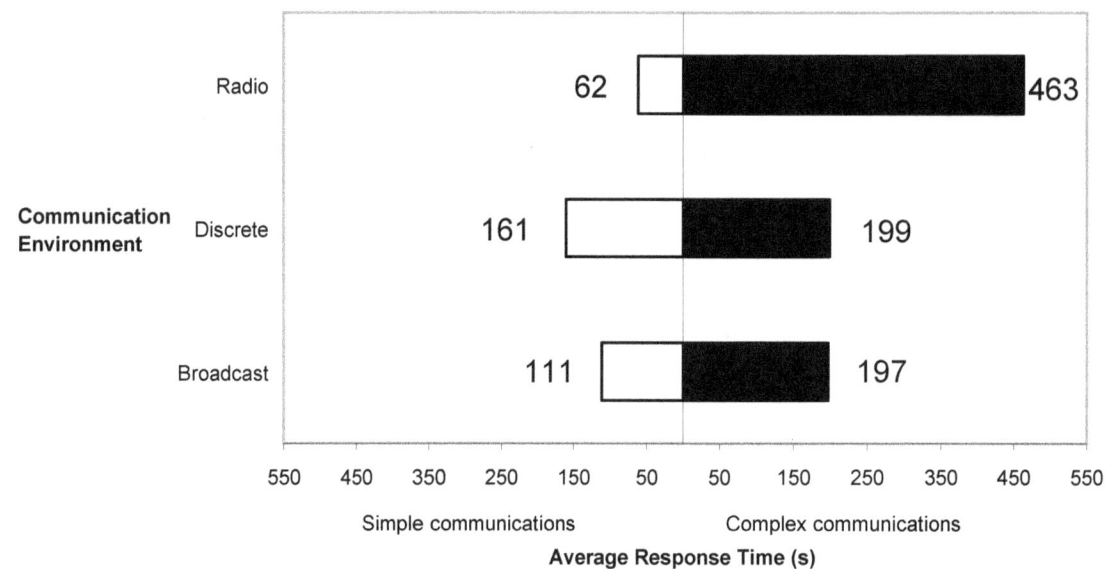

Figure 11. Mean Task Completion Time for Simple and Complex Type Messages by Communication Environment

In general, the differences in performance between voice radio and data link can be related to the way information in different sensory modalities is processed, and the design of the two communication interfaces. In the voice radio environment, information was presented in auditory form. In the data interface, information was presented in a visual form.

Van Cott and Kinkade (1972) provide guidance on message format. They indicate that short simple messages are more effectively presented in auditory form. Lengthy and complex messages are more effectively presented in visual form. Table 7, adapted from Van Cott and Kinkade shows the criteria for selecting the form information should take - either auditory or visual. In the voice radio environment, the simple messages met several of the criteria for selecting the auditory channel. The simple messages were generally short addressed events in time that needed to be acted upon immediately. By contrast, the complex messages were lengthy and needed to be available to the dispatcher for a longer period.

26

The advantage of the data link environments over the radio in processing complex messages can be attributed to the reduced memory needed to process information displayed visually. The data link systems gave a visual representation of train and MOW crew locations in text form and on the track layout display. MOW crews did not need to repeat which section of track was needed because of a failure to hear, transcribe, or understand the track section being described. The dispatcher could read the information in the text message or see the section requested on the track layout display color-coded in yellow.

Table 7. Characteristics for Selecting Modality in which to Present Information

Auditory	Visual
Simple	Complex
Short	Long
Message not referred to later	Message referred to later
Addresses events in time	Addresses events in space
Message acted upon immediately	Message not acted upon immediately
Visual system is overburdened	Auditory system is overburdened
Environment is too bright or dark adaptation is necessary	Environment is too noisy
Receiver must move about	Receiver remains stationary

Adapted from Van Cott and Kinkade (1972)

By contrast, the dispatcher in the voice radio environment dictated specific information to MOW workers when they were granted Foul Time (i.e., dispatcher name, date, time span granted, location, and number of work crew among others). While the dispatcher dictated the authority to work on the track, MOW people transcribed the information on paper. Then, the MOW person acknowledged the transmission by reading back that same information to the dispatcher. For Form Ds, dispatchers verified the readback by writing this information on paper. This process was time-consuming and prone to errors. With the data link interface, the dispatcher filled in the form directly on the computer and transmitted the message to the roadway worker. Upon receiving the message, the roadway worker read and acknowledged the message by sending a written confirmation back to the dispatcher. The time-consuming process of listening to the message and repeating it back to the sender was minimized because the visual display of the work authority was available to the dispatcher and could be acted upon more quickly.

Favorable comments by the dispatchers indicated that the visual representation of location information on the track layout display was particularly helpful in supporting the dispatcher's communication task, as well as managing the territory. The graphic representation lowered memory load by making information about the track visible over time. By displaying this information directly on the track display, the dispatcher could also see how it would impact the movement of trains or allocation of track to other MOW crews.

Specific aspects of the visual interface also facilitated the completion of complex transactions. During the design of the data link interface, interviews with dispatchers indicated they would not use an interface that required use of a keyboard to enter information. The development of message templates facilitated the data entry process. The dispatcher simply chose the appropriate message type from a menu of message types and filled in the key information. This procedure minimized transaction time by reducing the amount of data entry by the dispatcher. A system that required greater keyboard entry would have reduced the benefits of the visual interface compared to the auditory interface inherent with voice radio.

3.4   Situation Awareness

Table 8 shows the percentage of questions answered correctly, and summarizes the evaluation of situation awareness. While none of the differences between scores were statistically significant, an examination of the data is interesting. For voice radio, situation awareness scores were best for MOW activity followed by hazard awareness, communications, and routing. For both data link conditions, situation awareness scores were best for hazard awareness followed by MOW activity, communications, and routing. For both voice radio and data link conditions, routing ranked last. This finding suggests that dispatchers were devoting more resources to communication activities than to routing activities. Given the higher workload demands associated with this experiment compared to normal railroad operations, this seems reasonable. However, it is also reasonable to expect that the competition for visual resources in the data link condition by the visual presentation of text might result in a performance decrement in the data conditions compared to voice radio. Because vision requires selective attention, the dispatcher can focus on only one display at a time. However, a performance decrement for data link did not occur. Routing situation awareness scores were actually better in both data link conditions, although these differences were not statistically significant.

For three of the four activities measured, routing, hazard awareness, and communication performance were better with data link than with voice radio. The dispatchers demonstrated better knowledge of the train schedule, current train location, hazard location, and also when messages were sent and their content. Although the results were not statistically significant, the trend suggests that data link does not impair situation awareness compared to the use of voice radio. It may actually improve situation awareness.

Table 8. Situation Awareness by Activity and Communication Environment

| Activity | Percent Correct Response by Environment | | |
| | Voice Radio (%) | Data link | |
		Discrete (%)	Broadcast (%)
Routing	43	63	63
Hazards	57	85	74
Communication	56	71	66
MOW activity	82	85	72

A number of factors may have contributed to the improved performance trends in the data link conditions for these three measures. The visual persistence of messages enabled dispatchers to examine this information at their leisure while lowering memory load at the same time. Displaying information about routing and hazard location on the track layout display provided a method for relating this information to the train schedule. For example, in the data link conditions the dispatchers saw the hazardous area highlighted in yellow on the track layout display when they viewed the alerting message. In the voice radio environment, dispatchers relied on memory to retrieve this information. In current railroad operations, dispatchers write a personal note or report it in a "desk book." The visual display found in the data link interface saves time and resources by avoiding the process of putting this information in a visual form. By saving the cognitive and physical resources for other activities, dispatchers can devote more time to other tasks.

For MOW activity, situation awareness scores were similar for voice radio and data link conditions. Here, situation awareness for voice radio was slightly worse than the discrete condition and better than the broadcast condition. Of the four measures of situation awareness, MOW activity was the measure for which dispatchers showed the best performance in the voice radio condition. In the voice radio and data link conditions, the dispatcher made use of a visual display to process information about MOW activity. In current railroad operations, the dispatcher must prepare paperwork when granting a MOW request. This paper work (i.e., Form D) describes in visual form the track location and time for which the track authority is requested. In our experiment, dispatchers followed these procedures. Thus, the information received by voice radio was translated early on into a visual form. When the dispatcher put the MOW request into effect, this track authority was also displayed on the track layout display. This provided an additional visual cue, similar to what was displayed in the data link conditions. Thus, in both voice radio and data link conditions, a visual aid was available to assist the dispatcher.

These results suggest that data link does not impair situation awareness. Overall, a trend towards better situation awareness in the two data link conditions was observed compared to the voice radio condition. This improvement was attributed to the lower memory demands associated with information that was made available in visual form. Although the visual interface in the data link conditions increased attention to communication activities, routing situation awareness did not suffer.

3.5 Productivity

Two measures were used to assess productivity: the number of trains entering a station late (i.e., with a delay more than five minutes), and the number of MOW requests granted.

Table 9. Productivity by Communication Environment

	Environment		
		Data link	
Productivity Measure	Voice Radio (%)	Discrete (%)	Broadcast (%)
Late Trains	27	24	13
MOW requests granted	63	65	54

29

Table 9 shows the percent of trains more than five minutes late by environment and the percentage of MOW requests granted for each environment. For both measures, the results were not statistically significant. For both measures, the voice radio and the discrete data link environment show similar results. The broadcast data link condition shows the smallest percentage of late trains compared to the two other conditions. Having fewer alerting messages in the broadcast case might have lead to more free time to route trains. However, dispatchers granted fewer MOW requests in the broadcast condition. Overall, the data suggests that the data link interface did not adversely affect productivity compared to the voice radio interface.

3.6 Dispatchers' Preferences

The debriefing questionnaire gave the dispatchers an opportunity to comment on our data link designs as well as on the voice radio condition. Table 10 summarizes the answers to the debriefing questionnaires. The numbers in Table 10 represent average scores across participants on a scale from one to seven. A score of one represents a low or negative value (low workload, uncomfortable, unrealistic compared to revenue service). A score of seven represents a high or positive value (high workload, comfortable, realistic compared to revenue service). No statistically significant differences were observed.

Table 10. Dispatcher Ratings of Workload: Comfort and Simulator Realism

	Environment		
		Data link	
	Voice Radio	Discrete	Broadcast
Workload	6.3	6.0	5.8
Comfort	5.9	5.0	4.3
Realism	2.1	N/A	N/A

The dispatcher rated workload high in all three environments with an average score around six. The workload was perceived slightly lower in both data link environments. Dispatchers rated the realism of the voice radio environment 2.1 out of 7. Dispatchers commented, "No way is a territory that busy…" One dispatcher said, "No way can a man deal with that during eight hours. It is totally unrealistic." This rating can be attributed to the high workload. No dispatcher criticized the voice radio environment for lack of similarity with the current environment in respects other than workload.

All dispatchers felt relatively comfortable with the data link environments (see Table 10). Before the experiment began, most dispatchers expressed a negative attitude towards data link. However, after the experiment the dispatchers felt it would be very useful in addition to voice radio. The dispatchers also gave comments on the use and implementation of data link. These comments are summarized in Table 11.

Table 11. Dispatcher Comments on the Use of Data Link

Category	Comment
Choice of communication channel	Data link would be good for communicating TSRBs (with speed restrictions announcements), Form Ds for MOW crews and engineers, Foul Time, train crew and consist information, car placement information, planned track outage information, and emergency phone numbers.
	Choose voice radio for emergencies and when an immediate response is required.
Interface	A sound alert for incoming messages would be welcome in the data link environment.
	Provide capability to print paper copies of messages.
	Distinguish answered from unanswered messages.
	Use voice recognition.
	The highlighting feature makes a MOW request very clear, however, blocking actions should remove the yellow color code.
Safety	The dispatcher needs to know whether the recipient read the message. The acknowledgment procedure requires further work.
	When Foul Time is given back, dispatcher should acknowledge the message.
	Data link allows messages to be acknowledged when one has the time. There is no audio pressure to respond immediately.
	The broadcast feature could be misused in the same way as voice radio. MOW crews might take advantage of information about train and equipment movements to work without permission.

4. CONCLUSIONS

Voice radio congestion is a significant problem in the current dispatching environment. Data link has been proposed as an alternative communication channel to solve this problem. In particular, information presented orally over the radio can be presented in visual (text and graphic) or aural form with data link. The objective of this study was to evaluate how the introduction of data link technology might affect dispatcher performance. The results suggest that data link can improve communication efficiency without adversely affecting productivity, situation awareness, or safety. Even where the results were not statistically significant, they favored data link. Compared to voice radio, data link improved safety and situation awareness. For productivity, no statistically significant differences were observed between data link and voice radio.

Data link improved safety compared to the voice radio. In data link, dispatchers protected a greater percentage of trains and MOW crews compared to the voice radio. By providing information in a visual format, data link eliminated readback errors and hearback errors associated with the auditory modality. Eliminating these errors helped shorten the duration of complex, safety critical messages like temporary speed restrictions. Translating track requests from alphanumeric text to a graphic display on the track layout display made the request even easier to process. The visual nature of information presented in the data link systems reduced the demand placed on the dispatcher's memory. The dispatchers were much less likely to forget to respond to messages with data link than with voice radio. Anecdotal comments by the participants suggested it also reduced stress by providing a quieter environment in which to work, giving the dispatcher greater control over when messages were answered.

Communicating information in visual form did not negatively impact situation awareness scores. Where the differences between the data link and voice radio conditions were not statistically significant, the trends showed a positive impact for data link. Situation awareness scores for both data link conditions were better than voice radio for routing, hazard awareness, and communication. While the dispatcher devoted more resources to processing visual information with the data link conditions than with voice radio, (there were three displays to monitor instead of two), no adverse impact was evident. The dispatcher appeared to benefit by having a visually persistent display of information that reduced memory load. MOW activity was the only category in which performance was as good or better than the voice radio condition. Dispatchers had a visual form of information to assist them in situation awareness. In the voice radio condition, dispatchers wrote the track requests on paper as part of the track authorization process, which helped in acknowledging the request. This finding reinforces the importance of the visually persistent forms of information in supporting the dispatcher in processing complex information.

Overall, the differences between the discrete data link condition and the broadcast data link condition were small. The broadcast version showed a greater improvement in train safety than the discrete version. The broadcast version minimized communication workload by providing a simple way to reach multiple recipients and freed the dispatcher to attend to other tasks. For example, the dispatcher could use a single message to alert all trains along a particular branch. The discrete system required the dispatcher to contact each train individually.

However, implementing broadcast data link in revenue service will require addressing two issues related to information distribution and acknowledgment procedures. If a dispatcher failed to send a message as happened in one instance, or the message failed to reach the intended recipients, the consequences were larger since multiple parties were affected. Failure to send a single message placed multiple trains at risk. Thus, a single error can increase the risk of harm, compared to a system that only allows messages to be sent to one party at a time. System designers will need to consider how to minimize the impact of these types of errors.

A second issue for broadcast data link concerns acknowledging the receipt of messages. Acknowledgement means that the train crew has read and understood the message. Since dispatchers alert multiple trains simultaneously, they need to determine whether all trains received the message. Therefore, the dispatcher will need a method to keep track of acknowledgments. Designing the data link interface to support tracking of multiple acknowledgements will be an important requirement.

Communication efficiency for voice radio and the two data link conditions varied as a function of the characteristics of each medium. Information communicated by voice radio was presented in an auditory format. Information communicated via data link was presented in a visual format. Each form proved better suited for presenting some kinds of information than others. Voice radio proved to be better suited for communicating short and informal communications as well as time-critical messages that required immediate action (i.e., a dispatcher reporting no speed restrictions when a locomotive engineer called to request a temporary speed-restriction bulletin or alerting a locomotive engineer to the presence of a trespasser). For these types of communications, data link doubled the communication times over voice radio. These results were due to the auditory format in which the information was presented.

In this experiment, data link proved better suited for communications whose length or complexity imposed a significant burden on memory. In railroad operations, these characteristics are typical of safety critical messages that require formal acknowledgement procedures (i.e., granting a Foul Time request or authorizing a train movement using a Form D). Data link provided an efficient channel for these communications; transaction times were reduced by a factor of two. The idea of not having to repeat a message multiple times was also appealing to the dispatchers in our study.

In voice radio and data link conditions, the differences observed between the two types of messages were due to the modality or format in which the information was presented, not the communication medium. While information sent over the radio is presented in an auditory form, digital communications systems like data link afford more presentation options. Thus, data link supports both auditory and visual modalities. The properties listed in Table 7 suggest what format a message should take.

The differences identified between voice radio and data link also depended upon the details of how each interface was implemented. Had the data link interface required the dispatcher to make more use of the keyboard to enter messages than with the current design, the results might have been quite different. Pilot testing indicated that heavy use of a keyboard was unacceptable to the dispatcher population, and would have resulted in longer response times. Similarly, the ability to show track-related information in text or graphic format reduced communication errors and dispatcher response time. This feature also generated positive comments from the dispatchers. Successful implementation of a data link interface is dependent upon applying principles of good human factors design and usability testing to meet the needs of dispatchers who use this communication interface.

The current study suggests that dispatchers benefit from both voice radio and data link communication modes. In recommending the conditions under which medium should be used, this study suggests that voice radio is best suited for communicating simple, time-sensitive messages to one recipient. Data link system is best suited for communicating lengthy messages. Sending discrete messages works best where privacy is important or the message content would benefit only the recipient for which the message is intended. Sending broadcast messages works best when there is a need to communicate the same information to multiple recipients.

4.1   Future Research

This study suggests that data link technology has the potential to improve the safety and communication efficiency of the dispatching environment. However, the introduction of new technology and new interfaces raises new issues along with solving old problems. The current study compared voice radio to data link where each was the only medium. However, in actual operations both types of communication systems will be available. Currently, data link affords more flexibility in terms of how information is presented. The challenge for designers of future railroad communication and information systems will be deciding the format that different kinds of information should take.

As an example, consider the acknowledgment procedures for granting train movements or authorizing track use by MOW crews. For safety reasons, the acknowledgment procedure is needed to assure the sender that the message was received and understood. This issue is particularly important for messages concerning train movement authorization and track allocation procedures that are governed by formal operating procedures. The kinds of errors associated with the verbal acknowledgement procedures are less likely to occur when this information is presented in a visual format. Nevertheless, different methods of entering information (e.g., keyboard, mouse, or touch screen) will create new errors as well. Keyboard entry may result in transposition errors while mouse and touch screen entry may contribute to selection errors. Identifying these error types will be important to their mitigation.

Another example concerns how dispatchers allocate their attention to incoming messages. The temporal nature of messages received by voice radio calls for an immediate response by the dispatcher. In practice, however, the dispatcher does not immediately answer all calls (Roth, Malsch, and Multer, 2001). The dispatcher constantly evaluates whether to continue with the current task or switch to a different activity. When there is more than one call to answer, the dispatcher must decide which call will be attended to first. In this experiment, simples messages from train crews were acted upon more quickly than messages from MOW crews requesting track in the radio condition. This behavior was not observed with data link. Did the lower workload associated with granting a MOW request in the data link condition change how the dispatchers allocated their attention? How will dispatchers allocate their attention when voice radio and data link are used together? More research will be needed to understand how the use of both voice radio and data link impacts the dispatcher's attention allocation.

Several related challenges for designers will come from the increasing complexity of these information systems. By increasing the bandwidth over which information is communicated, data link will increase the quantity of information available to the dispatcher. To handle the increasing quantity of information, the interface for managing this information and railroad operations will also increase in complexity. Data link technology offers the ability to create public (shared) and private communication channels. What information should remain private and what information should be shared? For shared communication, how much information can be communicated before the operator becomes overloaded? How should the interface be designed to address information overload?

Both visual and auditory interfaces have limits to the amount of information that can be effectively displayed. Thus, large amounts of information may be hidden from the dispatcher. One challenge concerns getting lost in this information space (Elm and Woods, 1985; Woods, Roth, Stubler, and Mumaw, 1990; and Burns, 2000).

A second challenge concerns the management of the interface itself. As the information space increases in size, more cognitive resources will be devoted to dealing with the interface. Fewer resources will be devoted to cognitive activities directly associated with the operational task (e.g., deciding whether to authorize a train movement). Designers will need to carefully consider how the interface design impacts the dispatcher's ability to quickly find information so that attention remains on the operational task.

Finally, it is unclear from our results to what extent dispatchers are affected by the loss of information they acquire over voice radio that is not specifically directed to them. Roth, Malsch, and Multer (2001) observed that dispatchers in actual railroad operations took advantage of information overheard on the radio but not intended for them. The participants in this study did not appear to make use of this additional information. Further research will be necessary to determine the need for information now available through the party line and how that information could be provided in a data link system.

APPENDIX A. MESSAGE TREES

This appendix shows the message trees for the dispatcher and experimenter. In addition, the distribution list used by the dispatcher to specify the group of secondary recipients in the data link broadcast environment was included.

The Dispatcher Message Tree Used During the Experiment

High Priority
To Engineer- Fatalities

Trespasser hit	Train derailment
Notified RT – protection set up. Med. Assistance – help underway.	Notified RT help underway. To other trains – routing delays. To MOW – train derailed –busy time.

To Rescue Team

Trespasser hit	Train derailment
Alert rescue team.	Alert rescue team.

Medium Priority
To Engineer – Danger Warning

Trespasser	Obstruction – train stalled	Kids throwing stones
Trespassers on track ahead. Trespassers are gone. Trespassers have been taken care of.	Vehicle on track. Train stuck on track. Information request about stalled train. Locomotive is coming.	Kids are playing. Kids are gone.

To MOW –Danger Warning
NOW on the wrong track

Notification

Low Priority
To Engineer – Standard Communication

Temporary Speed Restrictions (TSR)	Track Problem	State of Engine	Special Train Movement
No TSRB TSRB follows TSRB update Special speed restrictions	Track repaired – reduced speed Track out of service – delay and reroute	Special routing due to risk of total failure	Special movement

Dispatcher to MOW – Standard Communication			*To Yard Routing preferences*	*To Lifting Bridge*
Track Work	Signal Work	Track Wishes	Need Locomotive	Bridge Lifting
Foul Time granted. Foul Time refused. Other Foul Time proposal Foul Time ends.	Foul Time granted. Foul Time denied.	Not possible – other track or wait. Okay for required track.	Can we have a locomotive?	Okay to lift bridge. Impossible to lift bridge.

Broadcast Group Selection
The broadcast group selection has two layers. The first layer is the type of recipient and the second is the location of these recipients. The broadcast group selection tree used in the experiment has the following structure:

(Recipient)   <u>Trains</u>
    (Location)   *On branch A*
                  On branch B
                  On branch C
                  On branch D
                  All

Trains and MOW
                  On branch A
                  On branch B
                  On branch C
                  On branch D
                  All

MOW
                  On branch A
                  On branch B
                  On branch C
                  On branch D
                  All

Everybody

Experimenter's Message Tree

ENGINEER MESSAGE TREE

<u>High priority</u>

Engineer to Dispatcher

Trespasser hit
- Train hit a trespasser
- Medical help is needed

Passenger dead/injured
- Assistance in station
- Assistance right away?

Train derailed
- Need help

<u>Medium priority</u>

Engineer to Dispatcher

Trespasser
- Seen on track

Engine failure
- Train stuck on track
- Freight train stuck
- Power insufficient – need power/loco

Threat for people in the train
- Chemicals released
- Bomb on the track

Kids throwing stones
- Kids throwing stones
- Not there any more

Obstruction
- Engine failure - train stuck on track
- Trees across the track
- No trees any more
- Additional locomotive needed – freight train

Failures
- Total power loss – Train stuck
- In cab system failure

Re-crewing
- Crew outlawed
- Re-crewing position OK

What is up?
- Need information – What are you doing?

<u>Low priority</u>

Engineer to Dispatcher

Engine state
- Engine OK
- Engine state – serious trouble

Track problem
- Track damaged

Bad weather
- Thunderstorm – reduce speed
- Leaves on the track – reduce speed

Special events
- Dignitaries on the train

Bulletin
    Bulletin request
Warning
    Long/large/high train!
Position report
    Current position
Engineer to Support staff
Engine state
    Engine OK
    Engine state – serious trouble

MISCELLANIOUS MESSAGE TREE
High priority

Police to Dispatcher
Police intervention
    Stop the train
    Corpse near the track
Rescue Team to dispatcher
Fatality
    Everything under control
Train derailment
    Everything under control
Passenger dead/injured
    Everything under control
MOW fatality/injury
    Everything under control
System to Dispatcher
MOW in danger
    Protection forgotten
    Gave Foul Time but unprotected!

Medium priority

System to Dispatcher
MOW person on the wrong track
    Worker not protected
Trespasser
    Trespasser on track
Obstruction
    Vehicle stranded on grade crossing
Unprotected station
    Station with no bridge crossing
Electrification problem
    Power cable failure
    Loss of electrification/power
Re-crewing
    Crew outlawed
Loco power problem
    Power insufficient
CETC problem
    Not updating – shift to radio communication
    Field signal problem – messaging routing

Electrification Department to Dispatcher
  Power loss
    Power outage on track.
    Power problem repaired

Low priority

System to Dispatcher
  Engine state
    Engine OK
    State of the engine – serious trouble
  Information
    Rescue operation – World information
    Unprotected station – World information
    Notified - Height limitation on given track
    Notified - Speed limitation on given track
    Emergency phone numbers
  Special events
    Dignitaries on train
    Special train
    Special car
  Delays
    Slow crew
    Scheduled meet not possible
  Bulletin
    Bulletin request
  Warnings
    Long/large/high train!
    Operation at limit capacity
    Reminder – Train priorities
    Signal workers on track
    Two meets and passes at same time
    Time to recover - alert
  Possible dispatching mistakes
    Omitted a warning
    Unnecessary route cleared
    Routing mistake – Lack of protection?
    Too much track given away
    Routing mistake – No power!
Yard to Dispatcher
  Train servicing
    Request particular track
System to Engineer
  Engine state
    Engine OK
    State of the engine – serious trouble
  Bulletin
    No bulletin
    Bulletin – restrictions
    Bulletin – update
Bridge Lifting to Dispatcher
  Bridge Lifting
    Ship waiting for bridge
    The ship passed

MOW MESSAGE TREE
<u>High priority</u>

    MOW to Dispatcher
        MOW fatality/injury
            Railroad person dead (heart attack)
            Medical assistance needed

<u>Medium Priority</u>

    MOW to Dispatcher
        Track Work
            Track Work permission request
            Track Work protection request
            Work completed
            Additional time requested
        Signal Work
            Signal Work permission request
            Signal Work protection request
        Track car failure
            Track car stuck
            Track car out of the way
        Track problem
            Track damaged
            Work performed – Speed restrictions
        Power loss
            Power outage on track.

APPENDIX B. EVENT SCHEDULES

Appendix B contains the schedules for the trains, hazards, and MOW work. The train schedule was provided to dispatchers during the experiment.

The following is the train schedule for Scenario #1

Br.	Dir.	Train #	Ptr.	Terminal		Interlocking		Interlocking		Interlocking		Interlocking		Interlocking	
BRANCH A	IN		1	1:26 PM	A1	1:23 PM	A2	1:21 PM	A3	1:14 PM	A4	1:07 PM	A5	1:00 PM	A-t3
			2	1:46 PM	A1	1:43 PM	A2	1:41 PM	A3	1:34 PM	A4	1:27 PM	A5	1:20 PM	A-t4
			3	2:17 PM	A1	2:14 PM	A2	2:12 PM	A3	2:05 PM	A4	1:58 PM	A5	1:51 PM	A-t2
	OUT	111	1	12:39 PM	A1	12:42 PM	A2	12:44 PM	A3	12:51 PM	A4	12:58 PM	A5	1:05 PM	A-t2
		113	3	12:58 PM	A1	1:01 PM	A2	1:03 PM	A3	1:10 PM	A4	1:17 PM	A5	1:24 PM	A-t1
		115	2	1:27 PM	A1	1:30 PM	A2	1:32 PM	A3	1:39 PM	A4	1:46 PM	A5	1:53 PM	A-t2
		117	3	1:34 PM	A1	1:37 PM	A2	1:39 PM	A3	1:46 PM	A4	1:53 PM	A5	2:00 PM	A-t1
BRANCH B	IN		6	1:42 PM	B1	1:38 PM	B2	1:32 PM	B3	1:27 PM					NS
			4	2:20 PM	B1	2:16 PM	B2	2:10 PM	B3	2:05 PM					NS
	OUT	221	3	12:50 PM	B1	12:54 PM	B2	1:00 PM					B4	1:05 PM	BL-t1
		223	6	1:06 PM	B1	1:10 PM	B2	1:16 PM					B4	1:21 PM	BL-t1
		225	5	1:27 PM	B1	1:31 PM	B2	1:37 PM					B4	1:42 PM	BL-t2
BRANCH C	IN		7	1:21 PM	C1	1:17 PM	C2	1:13 PM	C3	1:10 PM	C4	1:05 PM	C5	1:01 PM	No
			7	2:00 PM	C1	1:56 PM	C2	1:52 PM	C3	1:49 PM	C4	1:44 PM	C5	1:40 PM	No
	OUT	331	8	1:08 PM	C1	1:12 PM	C2	1:16 PM	C3	1:19 PM	C4	1:24 PM	C5	1:28 PM	No
		333	4	1:42 PM	C1	1:46 PM	C2	1:50 PM	C3	1:53 PM	C4	1:58 PM	C5	2:02 PM	No
BRANCH D	IN		8	1:35 PM	D1	1:33 PM	D2	1:25 PM	D3	1:21 PM	D4	1:17 PM	D5	1:10 PM	D-t1
			9	2:20 PM	D1	2:18 PM	D2	2:10 PM	D3	2:06 PM	D4	2:02 PM	D5	1:55 PM	D-t2
	OUT	441	8	12:42 PM	D1	12:44 PM	D2	12:52 PM	D3	12:56 PM	D4	1:00 PM	D5	1:07 PM	D-t2
		443	7	1:04 PM	D1	1:06 PM	D2	1:14 PM	D3	1:18 PM	D4	1:22 PM	D5	1:29 PM	D-t2
Yard	IN	225EQ	5	ar. 1:15 PM		To terminal									
	OUT	300EQ	7	ar. 1:30 PM		To Yard									

Station		Interlocking		Interlocking		Interlocking		Station		Interlocking		F.D.	Train #	Dir.	Br.
12:59 PM	A6	12:56 AM	A7	12:49 AM								1	100	IN	BRANCH A
1:19 PM	A6	1:09 PM	A7	1:02 PM								2	102		
1:50 PM	A6	1:44 PM	A7	1:37 PM								3	104		
1:16 PM	A6	1:18 PM	A7	1:25 PM										OUT	
1:29 PM	A6	1:31 PM	A7	1:38 PM											
1:56 PM	A6	1:58 PM	A7	2:05 PM											
2:04 PM	A6	2:06 PM	A7	2:13 PM											
			B6	1:26 PM	B7	1:19 PM	BR-t2	1:17 PM	B8	12:50 PM		6	200	IN	BRANCH B
			B6	2:04 PM	B7	1:57 PM	BR-t3	1:55 PM	B8	1:50 PM		4	202		
1:10 PM	B5	1:11 PM	B6	1:13 PM	B7	1:20 PM	NS-t3	1:22 PM	B8	1:24 PM				OUT	
1:23 PM	B5	1:24 PM	B6	1:26 PM	B7	1:33 PM	NS-t3	1:35 PM	B8	1:37 PM					
1:45 PM	B5	1:46 PM	B6	1:48 PM	B7	1:55 PM	NS-t3	1:57 PM	B8	1:59 PM					
												7	300	IN	BRANCH C
												7	302		
														OUT	
1:09 PM	D6	1:03 PM	D7	1:01 PM	D8	12:58 PM						7	400	IN	BRANCH D
1:54 PM	D6	1:49 PM	D7	1:46 PM	D8	1:43 PM							9	402		
1:18 PM	D6	1:18 PM	D7	1:21 PM	D8	1:24 PM									OUT	
1:32 PM	D6	1:32 PM	D7	1:35 PM	D8	1:38 PM										
										ar. 1:15 PM	5	225EQ	IN	Yard	
										ar. 1:30 PM	Yard	300EQ	OUT	

43

The following is the train schedule for Scenario #2

Br.	Dir.	Train #	Ptf.	Terminal		Interlocking		Interlocking		Interlocking		Interlocking		Interlocking	
BRANCH A	IN		1	4:31 PM	A1	4:28 PM	A2	4:26 PM	A3	4:19 PM	A4	4:12 PM	A5	4:05 PM	A-t3
			2	5:05 PM	A1	5:02 PM	A2	5:00 PM	A3	4:53 PM	A4	4:46 PM	A5	4:39 PM	At3
			1	5:32 PM	A1	5:29 PM	A2	5:27 PM	A3	5:20 PM	A4	5:13 PM	A5	5:06 PM	A-t3
	OUT	191	3	4:00 PM	A1	4:03 PM	A2	4:05 PM	A3	4:12 PM	A4	4:19 PM	A5	4:26 PM	A-t2
		193	2	4:32 PM	A1	4:35 PM	A2	4:37 PM	A3	4:44 PM	A4	4:51 PM	A5	4:58 PM	A-t1
BRANCH B	IN		3	4:19 PM	B1	4:15 PM	B2	4:09 PM	B3	4:04 PM					NS
			4	4:28 PM	B1	4:24 PM	B2	4:18 PM					B4	4:13 PM	BL-t1
			6	4:44 PM	B1	4:40 PM	B2	4:34 PM	B3	4:29 PM					NS
	OUT	291	4	4:01 PM	B1	4:05 PM	B2	4:11 PM	B3	4:16 PM					NS
		293	5	4:23 PM	B1	4:27 PM	B2	4:33 PM					B4	4:38 PM	BL-t2
BRANCH C	IN		8	4:27 PM	C1	4:23 PM	C2	4:19 PM	C3	4:16 PM	C4	4:11 PM	C5	4:07 PM	No
			7	4:37 PM	C1	4:33 PM	C2	4:29 PM	C3	4:26 PM	C4	4:21 PM	C5	4:17 PM	No
			8	4:58 PM	C1	4:54 PM	C2	4:50 PM	C3	4:47 PM	C4	4:42 PM	C5	4:38 PM	No
	OUT	391	8	4:03 PM	C1	4:07 PM	C2	4:11 PM	C3	4:14 PM	C4	4:19 PM	C5	4:23 PM	No
		393	7	4:22 PM	C1	4:26 PM	C2	4:30 PM	C3	4:33 PM	C4	4:38 PM	C5	4:42 PM	No
BRANCH D	IN		9	4:31 PM	D1	4:29 PM	D2	4:21 PM	D3	4:17 PM	D4	4:13 PM	D5	4:06 PM	D-t2
			10	4:54 PM	D1	4:52 PM	D2	4:44 PM	D3	4:40 PM	D4	4:36 PM	D5	4:29 PM	D-t1
			9	5:20 PM	D1	5:18 PM	D2	5:10 PM	D3	5:06 PM	D4	5:02 PM	D5	4:55 PM	D-t2
	OUT	491	8	3:54 PM	D1	3:56 PM	D2	4:04 PM	D3	4:08 PM	D4	4:12 PM	D5	4:19 PM	NS-t1
		493	9	4:20 PM	D1	4:22 PM	D2	4:30 PM	D3	4:34 PM	D4	4:38 PM	D5	4:45 PM	D-t2
Yard	OUT	360EQ	8	ar. 4:40 PM		To Yard									
		120EQ	1	ar. 4:40 PM		To Yard									

Station		Interlocking		Interlocking		Interlocking		Station		Interlocking	F.D.	Train #	Dir.	Br.
4:04 PM	A6	3:59 PM	A7	3:52 PM							1	120	IN	BRANCH A
4:38 PM	A6	4:31 PM	A7	4:24 PM							2	122		
5:05 PM	A6	4:57 PM	A7	4:50 PM							1	124		
4:35 PM	A6	4:37 PM	A7	4:44 PM									OUT	
5:00 PM	A6	5:02 PM	A7	5:09 PM										
			B6	4:03 PM	B7	3:56 PM	BR-t2	3:54 PM	B8	3:42 PM	3	240	IN	BRANCH B
4:12 PM	B5	4:09 PM	B6	4:08 PM	B7	4:01 PM	BR-t3	3:59 PM	B8	3:45 PM	4	242		
			B6	4:28 PM	B7	4:21 PM	BR-t3	4:19 PM	B8	4:10 PM	6	244		
			B6	4:17 PM	B7	4:24 PM	BR-t2	4:33 PM	B8	4:35 PM			OUT	
4:43 PM	B5	4:44 PM	B6	4:46 PM	B7	4:53 PM	BR-t3	4:56 PM	B8	4:58 PM				
											8	360	IN	BRANCH C
											7	362		
											8	364		
													OUT	
4:05 PM	D6	3:58 PM	D7	3:55 PM	D8	3:52 PM					9	480	IN	BRANCH D
4:28 PM	D6	4:19 PM	D7	4:16 PM	D8	4:13 PM					10	482		
4:54 PM	D6	4:49 PM	D7	4:46 PM	D8	4:43 PM					9	484		
4:20 PM	D6	4:20 PM	D7	4:23 PM	D8	4:26 PM							OUT	
4:50 PM	D6	4:50 PM	D7	4:53 PM	D8	4:56 PM								
										ar. 4:40 PM	Yard	360EQ	OUT	Yard
										ar. 4:40 PM	Yard	120EQ		

The following is the hazard schedule for scenario #1 (with MOW crew calling times). The gray area indicates the presence of a trespasser in a specific area of the track. Under each hazard are the identification numbers of the trains that would pass through this area if the trains ran on schedule. The first number in the gray area represents the number of the "alerter train"; the other numbers in the gray area represent the trains the dispatcher had to alert.

Time	Tresp.		Kids		Bridge	Messages	MOW	MOW out	Total Mess.
1:00 PM		221							
1:01 PM							SW #1		1
1:02 PM									
1:03 PM									
1:04 PM									
1:05 PM									
1:06 PM									
1:07 PM	100					1			2
1:08 PM									
1:09 PM									
1:10 PM					Disp	2			3
1:11 PM			300				RC #5		4
1:12 PM									
1:13 PM	113							SW #1	5
1:14 PM				443		3			6
1:15 PM							SW #3		7
1:16 PM		223	331			4			8
1:17 PM								RC #1	9
1:18 PM									
1:19 PM									
1:20 PM									
1:21 PM				400		5			10
1:22 PM									
1:23 PM									
1:24 PM							RC #6	RC #2	11,12
1:25 PM									
1:26 PM									
1:27 PM	102	200				6,7	RC #3		13,14,15
1:28 PM									
1:29 PM								SW #3	16
1:30 PM									
1:31 PM									
1:32 PM									
1:33 PM									
1:34 PM							TC #2		17
1:35 PM									
1:36 PM									
1:37 PM		225							
1:38 PM							SW #4		18
1:39 PM									
1:40 PM									
1:41 PM									
1:42 PM	115					8	TC #3		19,20
1:43 PM									
1:44 PM									
1:45 PM							RC #4		21
1:46 PM									
1:47 PM									
1:48 PM									
1:49 PM	117		302			9			22
1:50 PM			333		Disp	10			23
1:51 PM							SW #5		24
1:52 PM									
1:53 PM									
1:54 PM								TC #2	25
1:55 PM									
1:56 PM									
1:57 PM									
1:58 PM	104								
1:59 PM									
2:00 PM									

The following is the hazard schedule for scenario #2 (with MOW crew calling times)

Time	Tresp.		Kids		Bridge	Number of M	MOW	MOW End	Total Mess.
4:00 PM									
4:01 PM							SW #1		1
4:02 PM									
4:03 PM									
4:04 PM		240			491	1			2
4:05 PM							RC #2		3
4:06 PM									
4:07 PM									
4:08 PM								RC #1	4
4:09 PM									
4:10 PM					Disp	2			5
4:11 PM		291	391				RC #5		6
4:12 PM	120					3			7
4:13 PM		242							
4:14 PM									
4:15 PM	191						RC #3		8
4:16 PM									
4:17 PM			360	480		4.5		SW #1	9,10,11
4:18 PM									
4:19 PM									
4:20 PM									
4:21 PM								RC #6	12
4:22 PM									
4:23 PM									
4:24 PM									
4:25 PM							TC #2		13
4:26 PM									
4:27 PM			362						
4:28 PM									
4:29 PM			244			6	RC #8		14,15
4:30 PM			393	493					
4:31 PM									
4:32 PM									
4:33 PM			293						
4:34 PM									
4:35 PM							TC #1	RC #2	16,17
4:36 PM									
4:37 PM									
4:38 PM								RC #7	18
4:39 PM									
4:40 PM				482					
4:41 PM									
4:42 PM									
4:43 PM									
4:44 PM		293				7			19
4:45 PM							RC #4		20
4:46 PM	122					8			21
4:47 PM	193							RC #5	22
4:48 PM			364			9			23
4:49 PM									
4:50 PM					Disp	10			24
4:51 PM									
4:52 PM							TC #3		25
4:53 PM									
4:54 PM									
4:55 PM									
4:56 PM								TC #2	26
4:57 PM									
4:58 PM									
4:59 PM									
5:00 PM									

The following are the MOW schedules respectively for scenario #1 and scenario #2

Id - Scenario #1	where	asking	starting	ending	type
Repair Crew #1	before A3		0	17	FT
Repair Crew #2	between Term and B1		0	24	FT
Repair Crew #3	between B1 and B2	27	32	180	Form D
Repair Crew #4	between B3 and B6	45	50	90	FT
Repair Crew #5	before C2 and at C2	11	16	180	FT
Repair Crew #6	between C4 and C5	24	29	240	Form D
Track Car #2	before D2 and at D2	34	39	54	FT
Track Car #3	at D6	42	47	75	FT
Signal Worker #1	at B3	1	6	13	FT
Signal Worker #3	between D3 and D4	15	20	29	FT
Signal Worker #4	at C3	38	43	70	FT
Signal Worker #5	at B7	51	56	65	FT
bridge @10	between D7 and D8	20			
bridge @50	between D7 and D8	50			

Id - Scenario #2	where	asking	starting	ending	type
Repair Crew #1	between A2 and A3		0	8	FT
Repair Crew #2	between term and B1	5	10	35	FT
Repair Crew #3	between B1 and B2	15	20	120	Form D
Repair Crew #4	between B3 and B6	45	50	95	FT
Repair Crew #5	between C1 and C2	11	16	47	FT
Repair Crew #6	between C4 and C5		0	21	FT
Repair Crew #7	between D1 and D2	38	43	180	FT
Repair Crew #8	at C4	29	34	180	Form D
Track Car #1	and between D3 and D4	35	40	60	FT
Track Car #2	between D6 and D7	25	30	56	FT
Track Car #3	at B7	52	56	75	FT
Signal Worker #1	before station A	1	6	17	FT
bridge @10	between D7 and D8	20			
bridge @50	between D7 and D8	50			

APPENDIX C. QUESTIONNAIRES

Appendix C includes all the questionnaires: the situation awareness questionnaire, the post-experiment questionnaires for all three environments, and the final debriefing questionnaire.

Situation Awareness Questionnaire

Please answer the following questions as best as you can. Keep your answers as short as possible. You will have very little time and will not be allowed to use the dispatching system; hence, you are not expected to answer all questions properly.

1. What is the number of the most delayed train?
2. Can you estimate the time delay for that train?
3. What is the number of the least delayed train?
4. Can you estimate the time delay for that train?
5. When is your next train due out of the terminal?
6. Do you see any routing conflicts?
7. Do you have "hazards" somewhere on the territory?
8. Where?
9. Any particular restrictions on the track usage?
10. Where are your MOW crews?
11. Which MOW crew will complete its work next?
12. What track could you give away for a 15 minute span to a MOW crew?
13. Whom did you last talk to?
14. When did you last talk?
15. What was the subject of your communication?
16. What was the last message you heard that wasn't intended for you directly? (used only in the radio environment and in the DB environment)

Post Experiment Questionnaire

Radio environment

Please answer the following questions as best as you can. If you have any problems, we are here to help. Don't feel limited by the questions.

- Did you route before answering the messages, answer messages before routing, or neither – it depends on the situation?
- How realistic do you think the replica of the radio environment?

  Very Unrealistic   Very Realistic

  | 1 | 2 | 3 | 4 | 5 | 6 | 7 |
- How would you rank the workload during the experiment?

  Very Low   Very High

  | 1 | 2 | 3 | 4 | 5 | 6 | 7 |
- How comfortable were you in the radio communication environment?

  Very Uncomfortable   Very Comfortable

  | 1 | 2 | 3 | 4 | 5 | 6 | 7 |
- Any suggestions to make the system better. Improvements. Any comment is welcome. Feel free to write anything, especially critiques!

DD environment

- Would you like the data link directed environment in addition to your current radio environment? Why?[3]
- Did you route before answering the messages, answer messages before routing, or neither – it depends on the situation?
- How would you rank the workload during the experiment?

  Very Low   Very High

  | 1 | 2 | 3 | 4 | 5 | 6 | 7 |
- How comfortable did you feel with the data link directed system?

  Very Uncomfortable   Very Comfortable

  | 1 | 2 | 3 | 4 | 5 | 6 | 7 |
- How helpful would it be to have such data link capacities in your current environment?

  Very Unhelpful   Very Helpful

  | 1 | 2 | 3 | 4 | 5 | 6 | 7 |
- Any suggestions to make the system better. Improvements. Any comment is welcome. Feel free to write anything, especially critiques!

---

[3] The term discrete was used in place of directed in the body of the report because it more aptly describes the characteristics of this data link environment.

DB environment

- Would you like the data link broadcast environment in addition to your current radio environment? Why?
- Did you route before answering the messages, answer messages before routing, or neither – it depends on the situation?
- How would you rank the workload during the experiment?

Very Low						Very High
1	2	3	4	5	6	7

- How comfortable did you feel with the data link broadcast system?

Very Uncomfortable						Very Comfortable
1	2	3	4	5	6	7

- How helpful would it be to have such data link capacities in your current environment?

Very Unhelpful						Very Helpful
1	2	3	4	5	6	7

- Any suggestions to make the system better. Improvements. Any comment is welcome. Feel free to write anything, especially critiques!

Final Debriefing Questionnaire

Please answer the following questions as best as you can. If you have any problems, we are here to help. Don't feel limited by the questions.

- Which environment did you like most (Data link Directed, Data link Broadcast or radio)? Why?
- Would you like the data link directed system in addition to your current radio environment? Why?
- Could you please rank the following starting with the best?
    Radio only
    Data link Directed only
    Data link Broadcast only
    Radio and Data link Directed
    Radio and Data link Broadcast
- Would any environment be good for training? Why?
- Any suggestions to make the system better. Improvements. Any comment is welcome. Feel free to write anything, especially critiques!

APPENDIX D. EXPERIMENT DOCUMENTS

Appendix D contains all the documents provided to the dispatcher during the two one-hour experiments, except the train schedules and the message tree structure. Train schedules for the experiments can be found in Appendix B and the message tree structure can be found in Appendix A. In order, we have the explanatory text for the use of the simulator, the train schedule for the training scenario, the transfer sheets, the Form D sheets, and the Foul Time sheets.

Simulator quick user's manual

<u>About the routing:</u>

1. A red track is a track occupied by a train. When there is no train, the track is white.

2. Every train leaving the terminal has to be sent a bulletin before he/she can leave. Assume that, in any other station, the train has already started the ride and received a TSRB.

3. To clear the route, click first on the "clear route" button at the bottom of the screen. Then click on the entry and exit signals of the interlocking according to the route you want the train to take. The color of the track changes to green.

4. To unclear a route, click first on the "unclear" button at the bottom of the screen. Then click on entry or exit signal of the interlocking according to the route you want the train to take. The color of the track changes back to white.

5. The route will unclear automatically if a train has used it. The color of the track will change back to white.

6. To block a route for MOW activity, click first on the "block" button at the bottom of the screen. Then click on the part of the track you are giving away. You have to repeat the process if you want to block more track.

7. To unblock a route, click first on the "unblock" button at the bottom of the screen. Then click on the part of the track you want to unblock. You have to repeat the process if you want to unblock more track.

<u>Names:</u>

The territory has four main branches named A, B, C, and D respectively. Stations on these branches have the name of the branch. There are four stations: station A, station BR, station BL, and station D.

Interlockings have names composed of a letter (the branch) and a number, the number representing the order of the interlocking from left to right.

To identify blocks during communications, we use a set of three elements. First, the general position i.e. the interlocking, the station or interlockings on the left and on the right. Second, the number of the track - knowing that tracks are numbered from top to bottom and third, the number of the block.

About the messaging system:

1. The message console is divided in two parts: the left window handles received messages and the right window shows the messages that were sent out. In each of these windows, there are two elements: a list of all appropriate messages and the message, currently highlighted in the list displayed at the bottom of the window.

2. The dispatcher would answer a message by pressing the "send message" or "reply" button, and a list of preprogrammed messages will appear. These messages are sorted into a message tree. The tree has four levels: the priority, the recipient, the subject of the message and the preprogrammed message itself. A layout of the tree will be provided and explained to you.

3. To fill in the blanks in the messages, you can use either the keyboard or the mouse. Most blanks can be specified by double clicking on the adequate field and by clicking the target train or by using the keyboard directly (without double-click). This is valid for train numbers, MOW crew identifiers, and name of block to be worked on. The cursor automatically moves from one field to the next. When a message is highlighted, i.e., read, the blocks specified in the text of the message turn yellow on the routing screen.

About the work allocation:

There are two groups of messages related to work request. Each group is described below:

1. **Track work**- Track Cars or Repair Crews usually perform track work. We expect the dispatcher to answer their request using the correct branch of the message tree. The type of work will be indicated in the work request message.

2. **Signal work**- Signal Workers usually perform repairs on signal. They expect to receive answers from the signal work sub tree. Here again the type of work in the request message will help decide which branch of the tree to use.

About the message "replying," sending, and forwarding requirements:

1. Any update about hazards has to be transmitted to all other trains scheduled to ride the branch on which the hazard is located. These messages include: trespasser on the track and trespasser are gone, kids throwing stones and kids are gone, and finally, bad weather zone and bad weather zone is gone.

2. Overweight events and engine state messages are for your personal information.

Training Scenario Train Schedule

Br.	Dir.	Train #	Ptf.	Terminal	Interlocking		Interlocking		Interlocking		Interlocking		Interlocking		
Br. A	IN		1	1:26 PM	A1	1:23 PM	A2	1:21 PM	A3	1:14 PM	A4	1:07 PM	A5	1:00 PM	A-t2
	OUT	111	2	1:04 PM	A1	1:07 PM	A2	1:09 PM	A3	1:16 PM	A4	1:23 PM	A5	1:30 PM	A-t3
Br. B	IN		4	1:30 PM	B1	1:26 PM	B2	1:20 PM	B3	1:15 PM					NS
	OUT	221	5	1:07 PM	B1	1:11 PM	B2	1:17 PM					B4	1:22 PM	BL-t1
Br. C	IN		6	1:21 PM	C1	1:17 PM	C2	1:13 PM	C3	1:10 PM	C4	1:05 PM	C5	1:01 PM	No
	OUT	331	7	1:15 PM	C1	1:19 PM	C2	1:23 PM	C3	1:26 PM	C4	1:31 PM	C5	1:35 PM	No
Br. D	IN		9	1:35 PM	D1	1:33 PM	D2	1:25 PM	D3	1:21 PM	D4	1:17 PM	D5	1:10 PM	D-t2
	OUT	441	8	1:08 PM	D1	1:10 PM	D2	1:18 PM	D3	1:22 PM	D4	1:26 PM	D5	1:33 PM	D-t1
Yard	IN	331EQ	7	ar. 1:00 PM											

Station	Interlocking		Interlocking		Interlocking			Station	Interlocking		F.D.	Train #	Dir.	Br.
12:59 PM	A6	12:56 AM	A7	12:49 AM							1	100	IN	Br. A
1:34 PM	A6	1:36 PM	A7	1:43 PM									OUT	
			B6	1:14 PM	B7	1:07 PM	BR-t3	1:05 PM	B8	12:50 PM	4	200	IN	Br. B
1:27 PM	B5	1:28 PM	B6	1:30 PM	B7	1:37 PM	NS-t3	1:39 PM	B8	1:41 PM			OUT	
											6	300	IN	Br. C
													OUT	
1:09 PM	D6	1:04 PM	D7	1:01 PM	D8	12:58 PM					9	400	IN	Br. D
1:40 PM	D6	1:40 PM	D7	1:43 PM	D8	1:46 PM							OUT	
									ar. 1:00 PM		7	331EQ	IN	Yard

Transfer Sheets

Dispatchers take over the track given away by the previous dispatcher on the shift when they start their experiment. Dispatchers also get written information about the scheduled work during their shift. This information is usually found on a transfer sheet. The following are our transfer sheets (Note that the only similarity with the real world is the name and the type of information. The same is true for the Form Ds that follow.).

Transfer Sheet for scenario #1

Scheduled work information (provided when the dispatcher start the experiment):

1. Track outage is scheduled at 1:30 p.m. between interlocking B1 and B2 on track 1 and track 2 block 2, at interlocking B2 T11, at interlocking B2 T12, and at interlocking B2 T22 block 1. Repair Crew #3 will ask for protection around 1:25 p.m. Form D required.

2. Track outage is scheduled at 1:30 p.m. between interlocking C4 and C5 on track 3 block 1 and at interlocking C5 T33 block 1. The MOW crew will ask for protection around 1:25 p.m. Form D required.

Please follow the platform indications as closely as possible. As at South Station, some trains have a longer consist and might not fit everywhere. The schedule has been drafted accordingly.

Also, you might want to pay particular attention to the incoming train appearing during the simulation given that you don't have a big overview display.

Transfer Sheet for scenario #2

Scheduled work information (provided when the dispatcher starts the experiment):

1. Track outage is scheduled at 4:38 p.m. at interlocking C4 T32, interlocking C4 T22, block 2, and interlocking C4 T33, block 2. Repair Crew #8 will ask protection around 4:33 p.m. Form D is required in the radio environment.
2. Track outage is scheduled at 4:19 p.m. between interlocking B1 and B2 on track 3 block 1 and 2 and on track 4 block 1 and 2. Repair Crew will ask for protection around 4:15 p.m. Form D is required in the radio environment.

Please follow the platform indications as closely as possible. As at South Station, some trains have a longer consist and might not fit everywhere. The schedule has been drafted accordingly. Also, you might want to pay particular attention to the incoming train appearing during the simulation given that you don't have a big overview display.

Form D

Form D

Work Crew # _____

Date _____ Dispatcher's name _____

Starting Time _____ Ending Time_____

Location _____

_____

Foul Time form

Foul Time Request

Work Crew # _____

Date _____ Dispatcher's name _____

Starting Time _____ Ending Time_____

Location _____

_____

_____

GLOSSARY

Block: A length of track with defined limits on which train movements are governed by block signals, cab signals, or Form D.

Broadcast data link: A form of data link in which a message is sent to multiple designated parties.

Cognitive Task Analysis (CTA): Analysis of the cognitive demands of a complex task. This includes the knowledge, mental processes, and decisions that are required to perform the task. The goals of a CTA are (1) to identify what factors contribute to cognitive performance difficulty; (2) to uncover the knowledge and skills that expert practitioners have developed to cope with task demands; and (3) to specify ways to improve individual and team cognitive performance in a domain through new forms of training, user interfaces, or decision-aids.

Consist: The make-up of a train, including locomotives and cars. Also described by its locomotive power, tonnage, number, and type of cars, and location and type of hazardous materials.

Crossover: A combination of two switches connecting two adjacent tracks. When aligned, this switch combination allows movements to cross from one track to the other.

Centralized Traffic Control (CTC): A signal system that allows the dispatcher to know which blocks are occupied by trains and roadway workers, and to control switches and signals remotely from the dispatch center.

Data link: A digital communications capability which supports moving information between office-based and field-based computers and their operators. In the railroad environment, operators include: dispatchers, train crews, and roadway workers. Information is digitally coded and messages can be discretely addressed to individuals or multiple recipients. Information can be presented in multiple sensory modalities (e.g., visual or auditory).

Discrete data link: A form of data link in which a message is sent to a single party.

Form D: A track usage authority form that is issued by a railroad dispatcher. A Form D contains written authorization, restrictions, or instructions issued by the dispatcher to specified individuals. Form Ds permit trains and other track users to occupy specific segments of track identified by the railroad dispatcher.

Foul Time: Time during which track is temporarily obstructed for work on or around the track. The term "Foul Time" is used by railroads that follow the NORAC operating rules. Other railroads use different terms (e.g., track and time) to refer to the same condition.

Interlocking: A configuration of switches and signals interconnected to direct trains along different routes, the limits of which are governed by interlocking signals.

Maintenance-of-Way (MOW): On-track maintenance for repairing, testing, and inspecting track or wayside apparatus such as signals and communication devices.

NORAC: Northeast Operating Rules Advisory Committee.

Operating Rules: A book of rules that govern a particular railroad's operating procedures and practices.

Roadway worker: Any employee of a railroad or of a contractor to a railroad whose duties include the inspection, construction, maintenance or repair of railroad track, bridges, roadway, signal and communication systems and electric traction systems on or near the track. This definition also applies to employees or contractors who have the potential to foul the track and employees responsible for their protection.

Shunt: Activate automatic block or interlocking signals when present on track.

Territory: A section of railroad for which a dispatcher is responsible for the safe and efficient movement of trains and other on-track equipment.

TGV: Train à Grande Vitesse, the French high-speed train.

Track car: Equipment, other than trains, operated on a track for inspection or maintenance. Track cars might not shunt track circuits.

Track and Time: Time during which track is temporarily obstructed for work on or around the track. Other railroads use different terms (e.g., Foul Time) to refer to the same condition.

TSRB: Temporary Speed Restriction Bulletin(s).

REFERENCES

Association of American Railroads. (1996). *Railroad Facts*.

Basu, S. (1999). *Real time simulation of rail dispatcher operations*. Unpublished master's thesis, Massachusetts Institute of Technology, Cambridge, MA.

Burns, C.M. (2000) Putting it all together: Improving display integration in ecological displays. *Human Factors*, 226-241.

Devoe, D. B. (1974). *An analysis of the job of railroad train dispatcher*. Technical report, FRA-ORD&D-74-37, National Technical Information Service. Springfield, VA.

Ditmeyer, S. R., & Smith, M.. E. (1993, April). Data links and planning tools: Enhancing the ability to plan and manage train operations. *Rail International*, 69-77.

Elm, W.C., & Woods, D. D. (1985). Getting lost: A case study in interface design. *Proceedings of the Human Factors Society*, 29th Annual Meeting, pp. 927-931. Santa Monica, CA: Human Factors and Ergonomics Society.

Endsley, M. R. (1993). Situation awareness in dynamic human decision-making: Measurement. *Proceedings of the First International Conference on Situation Awareness in Complex Systems*, Orlando, FL.

Federal Railroad Administration. (2002). A Vision for the Future: Intelligent Railroad Systems *Five-Year Strategic Plan for Railroad Research, Development, and Demonstrations*. Report No. FRA/RDV-02/02 Washington, DC: U.S. Department of Transportation.

Golaszewski, R. (1989). An analysis of pilot-controller read-back errors. *Journal of Air Traffic Control*, October – December, pp. 53-56.

Igarashi, A. (1995, February). The new Shinkansen system. *Railroad International*, 18-34.

Lanzilotta, E. (1996). Dynamic risk estimation: Development of the safety state model and experimental application to high speed rail operation. Doctoral dissertation, Massachusetts Institute of Technology, Cambridge, MA.

Lindman, H. R. (1992). *Analysis of variance in experimental design*. Springer Verlag.

Martland, C. D. (1995). Modeling railroad line performance. *Railroad Application Special Interest Group (RASIG)*, 1995.

Monan, W. (1983). *Addressee errors in ATC communications: The call sign problem*. Report 166462. Moffett Field, CA: NASA Ames Research Center.

Monan, W. (1988). *Human factors in aviation operations: The hearback problem*. Report 177398. Moffett Field, CA: NASA Ames Research Center.

NORAC. (1997, January 1). NORAC operating rules and instructions. *Amtrak Northeast Corridor*, 6th Edition.

Parasuraman, R. (1997, June). Humans and automation: Use, misuse, disuse, and abuse. *Human Factors*, June 1997, 39 (2), 230-253.

Potter, S. S., Roth, E. M., Woods, D. D., & Elm, W. C. (1997, October). *Cognitive task analysis as bootstrapping multiple converging techniques*. Paper presented at the NATO-ONR Workshop on Cognitive Task Analysis, Washington, DC.

Reinach, S., Gertler, J., & Kuehn, G. (1997). *Training requirements for train dispatchers: Objectives, syllabi, and test designs*. Draft technical report, U.S. Department of Transportation, Federal Railroad Administration, Office of Research and Development.

Roth, E. M., Malsch, N. F., & Multer, J. (2001). *Understanding how railroad dispatchers manage and control trains: Results of a cognitive task analysis*. Report No. DOT/FRA/ORD-01/02. Washington, DC: U.S. Department of Transportation, Federal Railroad Administration.

Rumsey, A. F. (1997). Communications-based train control for rail transit systems. *Intelligent Transport Systems Quarterly*, Winter 1997 - Spring 1998 Issue.

Sano, H. (1998). COSMOS, Computerized safety maintenance and operation system of the Shinkansen. *COMPRAIL'98*, pp. 21-25, Lisbon, Portugal.

Sheridan, T. B. (1992). *Telerobotics, automation, and human supervisory control*. Cambridge: MIT press.

Van Cott, H.P., & Kinkade, R.G. (1972). *Human engineering guide to equipment design*. New York: McGraw Hill.

Vanderhorst, J. (1990, January). *ARES, for safety and service - A comparison of voice and data link communication in a railroad environment*. Burlington Northern Railroad Research and Development Department.

Vanderhorst, J. (1990, October). *ARES, for safety and service - A comparison of voice and data link communication: railroad dispatcher's perspective*. Burlington Northern Railroad Research and Development Department.

Vantuono, W. C. (1996). Communication based train control for transit: New York leads a revolution. *Railway Age*.

Veysseyre, R. (1995). Probabilités et statistique. *Polycopié de l'Ecole Centrale Paris*.

Woods, D. D., Roth, E.M., Stubler, W.F., & Mumaw. R. J. (1990). Navigating through large display networks in dynamic control applications. *Proceedings of the Human Factors Society 29th Annual Meeting*, 396-399. Santa Monica, CA: Human Factors and Ergonomics Society.